The Death of the Goddess

The Death of the Goddess
A Poem in Twelve Cantos

Patrick Colm Hogan

With an Introduction by
Rachel Fell McDermott

NEW YORK
www.2leafpress.org

2LEAF ✦ PRESS

P.O. Box 4378
Grand Central Station
New York, New York 10163-4378
editor@2leafpress.org
www.2leafpress.org

2LEAF PRESS
is an imprint of the
Intercultural Alliance of Artists & Scholars, Inc. (IAAS),
a NY-based nonprofit 501(c)(3) organization that promotes
multicultural literature and literacy.
www.theiaas.org

Library of Congress Control Number: 2014932364
ISBN-13: 978-1-940939-34-6 (Paperback)
ISBN-13: 978-1-940939-35-3 (eBook)

10   9   8   7   6   5   4   3   2   1

Published in the United States of America

First Edition | First Printing

2LEAF PRESS trade distribution is handled by University of Chicago Press
/ Chicago Distribution Center (www.press.uchicago.edu) 773.702.7010.
Titles are also available for corporate, premium, and special sales. Please
direct inquiries to the UCP Sales Department, 773.702.7248.

For Lalita

Patrick Colm Hogan

Table of Contents

ॐ

Patrick Colm Hogan

Acknowledgments

ॐ

MANY PEOPLE HAVE been generous with their time in reading and commenting on this poem at various stages. Gina Barreca was extremely kind and helpful—reading, commenting, suggesting. Wendy Doniger provided erudite support. Sharon Jessee helped sustain my commitment to the poem by teaching sections of it in one of her classes. Without the encouragement of Rachel McDermott, I may have given up on the poem. Frederick Aldama was, as usual, generous and thoughtful in moving the poem toward publication. Gabrielle David gave the poem a home. Most importantly, this poem never would have been begun without the wisdom and insight of my wife, Lalita Pandit Hogan, over many years. It would never have been completed without her reassurance and great aesthetic sensitivity. ॐ

Patrick Colm Hogan

Preface

ॐ

MYTH AND LIFE

Twenty-five or thirty years ago, I began reading ancient Indic stories of gods and goddesses, demons, sages, and ordinary people—stories from the Vedas (foundational Hindu religious texts) and the Purānas (collections of mythological tales). I was entranced, just as—a decade before that—I had been entranced by Vedāntic (ancient Hindu) metaphysics, doctrines regarding the nature of the soul and the universe. The variety and extent of publications in the area suggest that I am far from being alone in this fascination. Still, one might wonder what drew a Midwest-American student of English Modernism to fantastic tales composed thousands of miles and thousands of years away.

In at least some cases of this sort, there is a heritage-based reason for the engagement. My forebears, however, did not come from India. It is true that my wife is Indian, which perhaps gives me some vicarious familial link to Indic traditions. However, I am at best skeptical of heritage-based literary affiliations (including of course the heritage-based affiliations of European-Americans). Rather, I agree with Walter Benn Michaels that there is no particular reason for a person to assume he or she has special affinity with one author or body of literature due simply to the fact (or presumed fact) that his or her ancestors came from a particular place.[1]

More exactly, work in cognitive and social psychology suggests that we have a strong propensity to assume essential proper-

---

1 See his *The Trouble With Diversity: How We Learned to Love Identity and Ignore Inequality* (New York: Metropolitan Books, 2006). I should note that Michaels and I disagree starkly about the ongoing social impact of identity categories, such as race, even as we agree on the spuriousness of such categories.

ties for groups. The imputing of essences is commonly a matter of species. We view lions as having one essence, goldfish as having another. In practical terms, that works well enough, leading to appropriate differences in our behavior regarding lions and gold-fish. In the case of human groups, however, problems arise. We tend to assume unselfconsciously that social categories give the true nature of the group's members, that people sharing a national, racial, ethnic, or other socially consequential category share some sort of ontological status. That is what is at issue in heritage. One's "heritage" is defined by an identity category—national, religious, sexual, or whatever. For some reason, I have never had a strong sense of group belonging, and I have found it difficult to work up much enthusiasm for in-groups (or, in keeping with this, much antagonism toward out-groups). As a child of perhaps nine, I recall asking my father about rooting for sports teams. I reasoned that, if people want a team to win simply because it represents their home town, wasn't it right to root for the team from the bigger city, since a win for that team would make more people happy. Evidently, something was amiss, and not merely in my obliviousness to the widely discussed problems with pure Utilitarianism. By all criteria of psychological normalcy, I should simply have wanted the home team to win, rather than having to reason through just which team to support. In any case, the point illustrates my trouble with identity categories, including those that supposedly govern literary heritage. (We will return to this trouble in relation to the content of the Indic stories.)

Another way in which we might interpret engagement with myth and metaphysics is religious. If someone has mystical feelings of divine presence, then stories and doctrines relating to divinity might well engage and stimulate him or her. There is something of that in my case. I was brought up in a religious family and was in fact bothersomely devout as a child (witness my scrupulosity on the issue of sports fandom). One perhaps redeeming aspect of this spiritual orientation was my particular devotion to the Blessed Virgin. My dear, kindly (and playfully limerick-reciting) Uncle Erv – formally, Brother Paschal – was a Franciscan monk. He was associated with a shrine dedicated to Our Lady of Czestochowa, otherwise known as "The Black Madonna." When growing up, my primary image of Mary was not blonde-haired and blue-eyed, an idea that I continue to find alien and somehow implausible, even at an intuitive and emotional level. Her image was, instead, dark, with skin color and features that I would now think of as East African or South Indian (as well as two cuts into her right cheek, like scarification marks). It is no doubt the case that my reading about Hindu goddesses connected with my childhood devotion and my image of Mary. But today I am not religious at all. I do not believe in Hindu mythology any more than I believe in Christian mythology. Thus the emotional and imaginative impact of those stories cannot be a matter of religious devotion *per se.*

Another approach to the question might take up social context. In recent years, perhaps the fundamental cliché about culture and history is manifest in the practice of saying, not "culture" and "history," but "cultural difference" and "historical determination." The common presumption appears to be that cultures and historical periods are radically divergent from one another, that indeed to refer to culture or history at all is to refer to deep discontinuity. In this context, one might be drawn to another culture or historical period due precisely to its difference, its exoticism. Of course, no one would deny that there are differences across societies and times. Nor would anyone deny that difference plays a role in anyone's engagement with another culture – that is, a culture other than that in which one was raised. But the question is, just what the nature of that difference might be. In fact, far from profound or radical, cultural and historical differences appear to be more a matter of variations on common, human concerns. In this way, it seems more reasonable to refer to culturally particular patterns, rather than cultural difference – versions of shared motifs rather than bewildering and seductive Otherness.

In general, when I read Hindu myth and metaphysics – as when I read Sūfi Muslim mystical poetry, Yoruba folklore, and work in other traditions – what engages me most profoundly are the ways in which the stories and ideas speak to my own experiences, feelings, quandaries and conflicts. At their best, works in these traditions fill in something that was missing, something for which I had an emotional or imaginative need, only vaguely perceived before, but more fully recognized in retrospect. It is as if I have been observing some figure – an icon of great importance, an image bearing crucially on some part of my self or my social relations. But I have been confined only to a single viewing point, a limited perspective, with the figure fixed and immovable. Reading literature and philosophy from other traditions is not, to continue the analogy, a matter of looking at different icons, at other selves and social relations. It is the same icon all along, the same human self and the same human relations. But through the various traditions, that icon is loosed from its fixed place, lifted from behind a glass, as if I could now turn it in my hand and examine it from different angles.

I have felt this liberating effect most strongly with the Indic material. That is presumably due to the vast internal diversity of Hindu tradition. Though it is over-simple, one may roughly characterize different traditions as either exclusionary or incorporative. Monotheisms tend to be exclusionary. [2] They commonly make a sharp distinction between what may be accepted from other traditions and what may not, what is doctrinal and what is

---

2 Chinua Achebe suggests a similar point in his comments on Christian missionaries and the Igbo proverb, "Wherever something stands, something else will stand beside it," in conversation with Bill Moyers. See "Chinua Achebe" in Moyers' *A World of Ideas: Conversations With Thoughtful Men and Women About American Life Today and the Ideas Shaping Our Future,* ed. Betty Sue Flowers (New York: Doubleday, 1989), 333-44. (The interview is available online at http://www. youtube.com/watch?v=_FzVUXxqNdw [accessed 20 January 2014].)

not. Hindu tradition, in contrast, tends to be strikingly incorporative. For example, many Hindus are perfectly willing to accept Jesus as an incarnation of Vishnu, along with Krishna, Rāma, and so on. Christians, however, are unlikely to see Krishna and Rāma as incarnations of God the Son – or, if they do, they are likely to be viewed as not really Christian. This diversity of Hinduism is well represented in the Vedas and, even more, the Purānas. Of course, there are complications here. Hindu diversity is currently threatened by self-proclaimed defenders of Hinduism who want to make it into a dogmatic monotheism, rejecting its characteristic variety and range. Moreover, there have been exclusionary sectarian squabbles within Hinduism from before the time anyone thought of the tradition as "Hinduism."[3] Conversely, there are incorporative strains within Christianity, Judaism, and Islam.

Indeed, in keeping with this final point, one might argue that Marianism is, in effect, a somewhat muted form of goddess worship that has managed to maintain a place within Catholicism. This makes further sense of the link between my early childhood devotions and my engagement with Hindu goddess myths. The Purānas take up goddess devotion, to which I was clearly drawn, but provide a far less emotionally circumscribed and far more imaginatively elaborated set of narratives treating female divinity. Indeed, construed in this way, we have a clue as to why I might have felt a retrospective need for something like a goddess mythology and why the Purānas may have satisfied that need. Given my current beliefs, this need was not religious *per se*. But religion itself satisfies some emotional and imaginative wants that are more mundane and personal. In my case, those wants found their first, partial satisfaction in Marianism. But Mary is a simplified figure in comparison with the multiform goddess of Hindu stories – a figure who can be an all-understanding mother or a neglectful one, a gentle or withdrawing spouse, a sacrificial victim or a warrior.

---

3 See, for example, the conflicts in Bhatta Jayánta's *Much Ado About Religion,* ed. and trans. Csaba Dezső (New York: New York University Press, 2005).

Thus, we begin to see why the myths might have appealed to me. They touched on some lack or absence that had been filled in childhood by devotion to the Blessed Virgin – not the religious commitment as such, but what underlay it. Moreover, they rendered the imagination of that devotion more complex and thus more adaptable to the complexities of my experience and my emotional responses to that experience.

Yet this personal explanation leads to another question. Many people are drawn to Indic mythology; can this just be coincidental or are the reasons the same? In other words, to what extent are my responses generalizable? I suspect that the answer to the latter question is – partially, but not wholly. There would be no such thing as Marianism within the Catholic Church if devotion to the Blessed Virgin had attracted only me. Moreover, the point is not confined to Catholicism. There are developments within Islamic mysticism and within Judaism that suggest members of those confessions too have felt that there was something missing in patriarchal monotheism. Again, the point is not precisely a religious one. It is, rather, a matter of what underlies religion, what needs religion itself satisfies. This only leads us into a further quandary – what, then, are those underlying needs?

It has been a commonplace for some time that religion serves to give pre-scientific explanations for natural phenomena. This is undoubtedly true, but it tells us only about a very limited part of religion. Saying that religion explains human tragedy goes further, helping to account for petitionary prayer ("Please, God, don't let..."). But this too does not have great psychological depth. The most engaging and inspiring myths go well beyond explaining why the leopard has spots or even why there are labor pains or the need for work. What engages us in a myth is only occasionally the conclusion. This is illustrated by the fact that myths continue to enthrall many readers who do not in any way believe in the explanations they furnish. Instead, both literature and myth, it seems, respond to some impulse connected with re-imagining the world, often in ways that we might characterize as metaphorical, and with experiencing a range of feelings connected with that imagination—and with the real world conditions and events that the imaginations vary. Specifically, our emotional and practical lives—especially our bonding relations (the love of spouses, parents and children, or friends)—give rise to interests, hopes, and anxieties that baffle and frustrate us. The imaginative simulations of literature and myth respond in part to that sense of bafflement and frustration, working out some of its apparently anomalous complexities. In keeping with this, bonding and the uncertainties of bonding are at the center of this poem—parental and filial bonds, bonds of friendship, and romantic bonds, depending on the characters and their situation.

Yet, once again, this leads us to a question: Just how does myth—goddess myth or any other—respond to our bafflement and frustration? It seems that it does this in part emotionally and in part intellectually. Emotionally, it may fill us with the joys of beauty, including the terrible joys of sublimity, which is to say tragic beauty. Intellectually, it does so by presenting us with ways of thinking about and perhaps better understanding our own lives. This is not to say that it teaches us straightforward lessons. Myths rarely have isolable morals in the manner of fables. Moreover, even with fables, the morals usually simplify the story, even to the point of occluding its ethical subtleties and, so to speak, blunting its moral edge. Rather, myths present us with models that we may use as structures for comparison, helping us at least at times to think about our lives in more intricate and nuanced ways.

In my case, there seems to have been a felt need for the beauty and sublimity of the goddess narratives (incompletely present in the Marianism of my childhood) and, beneath that, for ways of thinking about and responding to conflicted and disheartening particulars in my own life. Those particulars might include, for instance, a keen sensitivity to attachment separation, presumably related to early childhood experiences. Such particulars are also likely to be partially, but not wholly generalizable. To some extent, the bafflements and frustrations in my life are idiosyncratic. Yet, to some extent, they are the sorts of problem faced by many people. Moreover, many of the concerns that I encountered in myths were not simply personal, even if widely shared (e.g., grief over lost or endangered human bonds). Rather, they had broad social or political implications as well. Both these aspects are important, separately and in relation to one another. Without personal resonance, the issues suggested by the stories would be lifeless, mere abstract topics, not deeply felt concerns. But without the political and social implications, experiential preoccupations risk triviality, reducing to matters of personal vanity.

The issue of generality became particularly consequential when, about two decades ago, I began reshaping the Purānic myths and Vedic stories—along with Christian narratives, Sūfī motifs, Yoruba and Igbo folk traditions, and other sources—into a narrative poem that addresses problems that are both personal and political. After many drafts and revisions, that narrative poem became *The Death of the Goddess*.

In part, the poem seeks to revise or re-envision the source myths and to extend their modeling function more fully to social and political issues, particularly one fundamental social and political issue—the division of society by identity categories, an issue we have already touched on briefly. A good deal of empirical research shows that our inclination to divide society by identity categories, to organize our social lives into in-groups and out-groups, is robust, and destructive. We undervalue out-group members in a range of ways, even to the point of dehumanizing them.[4] This dehumanization is often manifest in the assimilation

---

4 On dehumanization, out-grouping, and demonization, see my *The Culture of Conformism: Understanding Social Consent* (Durham, NC: Duke University Press, 2001), especially 91-100 and 140-147.

of out-groups to devils—as in Nazi propaganda regarding Jews. This tendency furnishes a central metaphor in the poem, where the most oppressed groups are classed as demons. The point is in keeping with Indic traditions, where enemies have commonly been identified as "rākshasas" or demons. The poem represents these demons as the most ethical and humane group. This is in keeping with empirical research showing that "the perception that they are in a lower class can increase . . . the likelihood that [people] will behave compassionately and prosocially." Conversely, "the perception that they are in an upper class can . . . lower willingness to observe ethical norms." [5]

In the ancient, Indic context, the most fundamental identity-group oppositions were a matter of caste. Thus I frequently draw on caste ideas and practices in the course of the poem, particularly ideas and practices relating to Untouchability, the most severe and debilitating form of caste oppression. But this is not, in the first place, a critique of the caste system. It is, rather, the deployment of a critique of caste—a critique drawn substantially from Indic traditions themselves—to suggest ways of thinking about and opposing other forms of identity-group oppression. The broad social dynamics of the caste system help us to understand and rethink different sorts of in-group/out-group divisions, such as those based on race (as in American slavery or segregation, or South African Apartheid), ethnicity (as in the Holocaust), or religion (as in Islamophobia).

One of the things that is fascinating about ancient Indic traditions is that they include strict caste divisions along with systematic opposition to caste. That opposition may be found in Buddhism, Jainism, and Hinduism itself. For example, according to the *Brihadarānyaka Upanishad,* when one realizes "the self,"

---

5 Peter Belmi and Margaret Neale, "Mirror, mirror on the wall, who's the fairest of them all? Thinking that one is attractive increases the tendency to support inequality," *Organizational Behavior and Human Decision Processes 124* (2014): 133-149.

then "an outcaste is not an outcaste, a pariah is not a pariah."[6] (The Upanishads are among the founding religious texts of Hinduism.) The key point of conflict within Hindu tradition is straightforward. One fundamental precept of Vedāntic thought (thought derived from the Upanishads) is that each individual soul ("ātman") is the all-encompassing God or spiritual Absolute ("brahman") and that changeable particularity and difference are merely illusion ("māyā"). (Realization of this identity is called "release" or "liberation," as it ends one's painful, desirous attachment to illusion.) But if this is the case, then it necessarily follows that the soul of a high caste person and the soul of a low caste person are in fact the same, that they are both instances of God, and that the apparent differences between them—including differences in caste—are merely illusory. The idea appears both in philosophy and in narrative. For example, one Shaivite treatise forbids the devotee from practicing caste divisions, condemning anyone who does.[7] (Shaivites are devotees of Shiva.) In keeping with this, narratives of Shiva link him with Untouchables at the lowest rung of the caste hierarchy.

The point is worked out in ancient Indian ethical theory as well.[8] There is a fundamental ethical division between personal duty ("swadharma") and universal duty ("sādhāranadharma"). Personal duty includes abiding by one's caste rules. These caste rules may involve the perpetration of violence or deceit. In contrast, universal duty involves adherence to general standards, including a commitment to non-violence ("ahimsā") and truth ("satya"). Thus in ethics as well as in metaphysics and myth, Hindu traditions face the reader with a stark contradiction between the

---

6 In Patrick Olivelle, ed. and trans., *Upanisads* (Oxford: Oxford University Press, 1996), 61.

7 *Mahānirvāna Tantra* in Wendy O'Flaherty, ed. and trans., *Textual Sources for the Study of Hinduism* (Chicago, IL: University of Chicago Press, 1988), 137.

8 On the varieties of dharma, see, for example, Wendy Doniger O'Flaherty and J. Duncan M. Derrett, eds. *The Concept of Duty in South Asia* (New Delhi, India: Vikas Publishing, 1978).

principles and practices of hierarchical identity-group divisions and the principles and practices that go against such hierarchical divisions. Readers familiar with Gandhi's politics will recognize that this opposition has been directly carried into the modern period with Gandhi's deployment of ahimsā ("nonviolence") and satyāgraha ("insistence on truth") in struggles for national independence and social reform. This link with the modern period is central to the following poem.

In addition to Gandhian activism, *The Death of the Goddess* bears on a range of violent and oppressive identity conflicts from the modern period, the time when, as Ashis Nandy put it, "human destructiveness reached its creative pinnacle." [9] These include cases already mentioned – American slavery and subsequent racial discrimination, the Holocaust, and Islamophobia – as well as a range of other horrors from World War I to the Vietnam War, from colonial conquests to the cruelties of newly independent states (such as the Partition violence in India and Pakistan). The poem does not deal with these topics directly, but rather alludes to, for example, Nazi racial theory or South African gold mining – or other terrors, such as Soviet show trials – to suggest how the re-envisioned myths may offer ways of thinking about these and related atrocities.

Consider, for example, a small, embedded story included in canto eleven. One of the goons who has taken on the job of punishing the goddess retells the story of a servant who violates rules of social hierarchy and is therefore killed. Just before he dies, we are told, the servant thanks his executioner. As used here, the story has several points. It suggests the degree to which violence is a function of unjust hierarchies, and the degree to which such hierarchies accustom us to cruelty. It also suggests either

9 "Violence and Creativity in the Late Twentieth Century: Rabindranath Tagore and the Problem of Testimony," in *Rabindranath Tagore: Universality and Tradition,* ed. Patrick Colm Hogan and Lalita Pandit (Madison, NJ: Fairleigh Dickinson University Press, 2003), 264-281.

the unscrupulous propaganda undertaken by dominant groups (who lie about their victims' attitudes) or the psychological devastation wrought on oppressed people (who may come to see their own pursuit of justice as sinful) – or, what is most likely, both. The story gives us a little model for thinking about issues ranging from the trustworthiness of official histories (including our own) to the dynamics of torture and confession – a sadly pressing issue in the United States today. The main source of the story is found in the *Rāmāyana*. However, the basic idea recurs in other literary traditions as well. In the West, one may cite cases ranging from the Shakespeare's *Henry V* to Orwell's 1984. In the former, one rebel says "God be thanked" for preventing the rebellion's success, while another proclaims, "Never did faithful subject more rejoice / At the discovery of most dangerous treason," which "Prevented a damned enterprise."[10] In Orwell's novel, Parsons – a committed Party member – is arrested for muttering something in his sleep. In prison, he has no doubt that he is guilty of "thoughtcrime" and explains, "I'm glad they got me before it went any further."[11]

In sum, the poem draws on ancient Indic myths and philosophies, synthesizing these with related narratives and motifs from other traditions. It sets out to re-imagine these sources in such a way as to enhance and specify their personal concerns, primarily concerns of bonding. It focuses particularly on how personal relations are deformed or broken by modern and contemporary social and political conflicts, and cruelties bound up with identity categories. In doing this, it aims at fostering renewed and variegated reflection on those conflicts, cruelties, and (putative) identities.

---

10 *The Life of King Henry the Fifth* (II.ii.158, 161-162, 164), in *The Complete Works of Shakespeare*, 4th ed., ed. David Bevington (New York: HarperCollins, 1992), 852-892.

11 George Orwell, *Nineteen Eighty-Four* (Fairfield, IA: 1st World Library, 2004), 290, 291.

On the other hand, this work is, first of all, a poem. In that sense, its primary purpose is not ethical or political, but aesthetic. As such, it involves systematic attention to the development of metaphor, simile, and other figures, as well to the sound and rhythmic patterns—the music—of the verse. I have not emphasized this in the foregoing comments as the poetic purposes of the work should be more readily accessible without introduction. Nonetheless, it may be helpful to note two of the more important formal features. First, rather than either free verse or strict meter, the poem has a loose structure of five major stresses or beats per line. Knowing this may help readers pick up the cadence of the verse. Second, rather than either ordinary speech or a strict genre pattern, it includes a great deal of assonance, alliteration, and internal rhyme, which are recognizable—particularly when read aloud—but not predictable beforehand. In these ways, the form of the poem combines some of the systematic musical patterning found in traditional verse, but it moves toward free verse in rejecting the narrow constraints of a single, formal template.

Finally, to help orient the reader, I should say something about the identification of the characters in the poem. There are six major characters, all referred to by epithets rather than proper names. These are Grandfather, Grandmother, the Savior, Slave of Time, and, most important, the God of Tears and Little Mother (the Goddess of the poem's title). All are deities with many alternative epithets, except the sometimes demon and sometimes human Slave of Time. There are minor characters as well, such as the horse-bodied twins, Ritual Fire (alternatively, Sacred Pyre), and God of Exact Rites (equivalently, Father of Sacrifice). The various deities are recognizably drawn from Purānic and Vedic prototypes. However, I have avoided proper names, since their characterization has been so altered that it would be wrong to identify any of them with a specific Hindu deity. In order to help the reader keep track of the characters, the following list of alternative epithets may be helpful.

THE DEATH OF THE GODDESS

Little Mother, The Goddess, Destroyer of Illusion, Ethereal Goddess, Everything-that's-Fierce, Fierce Nature, Fierce One, Food-Giver, Goddess of Eternal Night, Goddess of Tears, Illusion's Foe, Last-Born Girl, Little Beauty, Ma, Mother of All, Night of Death, Night of Love, Our Little Girl, Peace of the Night, Queen of Beggars, Sacrifice, Savage, Unmoving Goddess, Unreachable, Virgin Goddess, Virgin-Girl

God of Tears, Champion in Thirst, Conqueror of Death, Consoler of the Enemy, Count-My-Bones, Emblem of Chastity, Face of Famine, Fearless One, Friend of Outcastes, Ghostface, Giver of Joy, God of Anger, God of Dance, God of Dreams, God of the Left Hand, Howler, Icon of Hunger, Image of Hunger, Knobby-Knees, Lefty, Leperskin, Little-Dollop-of-Ingudi-Oil, Little-Sack-of-Ribs, Lord of Rags and Ashes, Lord of Sorrow, Lord of Yoga, Mad One, Oddball, Poison-Drinker, Pretzel Legs, Remover, Skinny Boy, Smelly Clod, Source of Fire and Rain, the Friend, Top Dog of Ascetics

Grandfather, Eternal Home, First God, Great Origin, Immensity, Shaper of Life and Death, Source of All

Grandmother, Flowing Spring, Giver of Speech, Goddess of Rivers, Lotus Cradled, Moon Crescent, Source of Knowledge

Savior, Absolute Protector, Beloved Son, Compatriot, Dear Son, Demon-Strangler, Eternal Ally, Protector of the Faith, Redeemer, Right Arm of Faith

I should also warn the reader that the poem develops a self-consciously contradictory metaphysics with respect to these characters. On the one hand, the entire world is simply the dream of Grandfather; on the other hand, the ultimate reality is the undifferentiated union of the God of Tears and Little Mother. On the one hand, Little Mother is born last of all the gods and goddesses; on the other hand, she is the source of everything, even of Grandfather and the God of Tears. There are many paradoxes of this sort developed in the poem. Though they derive from principles of Vedāntic metaphysics, they are not simply riddles that conceal a clever resolution. If successful, they operate to foster and complicate cognitive and emotional response, like the story models they encompass.[12] In other words, the paradoxes do not so much mean something as (I hope) do something. In this sense, they are exemplary of the poem as a whole – and, more generally, of the complex and dynamic relation between myth and life.

—Patrick Colm Hogan
Mansfield, CT
January 2014

---

12 Writing in a different, but not unrelated context, Wendy Steiner has stressed the "paradoxical nature" of art as what "permits us to enter a fictive work and adapt it to the real needs and interests of the moment, to achieve insight into reality by freeing us from real constraints" (*The Scandal of Pleasure: Art in an Age of Fundamentalism* [Chicago, IL: University of Chicago Press, 1995], 80)—or, one might say, by provoking reflection on what we had previously assumed about such constraints.

Introduction

૭

SINGING PAIN

THIS POEM BY PATRICK COLM HOGAN, loosely based on the Hindu story of Siva and his wife Sati, is a text of terror. No one who has read it will ever again be able to think that Hindu myths about battles between gods and demons are just stock images, the obligatory "good versus evil" backdrops for salutary stories of gods and goddesses who bring succor and salvation to the world. Many of us are used to reading in such myths that the earth trembles under the weight of the carnage inflicted by the evil of the demons, or that the gods go to Lord Brahma, Vishnu, or Shiva to beg for aid, or that the gods and demons become puffed up with a pride that leads to their downfall. We tend to think of such descriptions as bloodless, as occurring in a heavenly realm that does not really concern us. No more. As the Goddess says, "on earth, as always, things are worse" (p. 63). The first time I began to read *The Death of the Goddess* I was so disturbed by the reality of the imagery in the poem that I could not sleep and could not finish the text. Patrick Colm Hogan knows what many of us never acknowledge in our encounter with myths: that the gods and demons are patterned on, are ciphers for, human depredation and wretchedness. To understand why the Goddess matters, why her death is both tragic and redemptive, we have to see ourselves and our human history as Hogan does. And for someone expecting a soothing retelling of a beloved myth, this is a shock.

Although Hogan explains that the characters in *Death of the Goddess* do not necessarily represent known Hindu gods and goddesses, for someone familiar with the stories of Brahma, Vishnu, Shiva, and Shiva's wife Sati, daughter of Daksha, the poem makes fascinating reading. If one had to categorize the tenor of the poem along traditional sectarian lines, one would say that the author is a Shakta-Shaivite, and that what Hogan celebrates about Shiva and the Goddess are their championing of the downtrodden, the poor, the Untouchable, and the maimed and dying. Shiva and the Goddess, or, as he calls them, the God of Tears and the Little Mother, descend to the level of those they care for; they weep over them, they take their parts, and they die for them, with them, and as one of them. Shiva is known by a number of splendid epithets: some recall traditional Puranic stories (God of Dance, Lord of Yoga, and Poison-Drinker), others bring to mind accusations leveled against him by "respectable" deities in the Puranas (Howler, Lord of Rags and Ashes, Mad One), and still others are unique to Hogan (for example, Count-My-Bones, Friend of Outcastes, Ghostface, Knobby-Knees, Leperskin, Oddball, Pretzel Legs, and Smelly Clod). Shiva accepts everyone, and he is the only character in the story (and, apparently, in the heavenly world), to treat his wife as equal to himself (p. 81). To help the ungrateful gods, who do not even bother to thank him, Shiva swallows the poison of their lust and evil deeds. Hogan makes us stop here. Do not think of a lovely blue-throated Siva, as we are used to in glossy modern calendar art, but of the slow and agonized death of an Indian farmer who has consumed pesticide in his despair. This is the sacrifice Shiva makes.

Vishnu, whom Hogan perhaps ironically calls the Savior, the Beloved Son, and the Protector of the Faith, is taught lessons in "The Death of the Goddess." Vishnu is unwilling to break the rules of social hierarchy for healing until the end of the poem, when he admits that "in structuring society by rank/ according to imaginary grades of good/ we have destroyed ourselves, and spoiled/ whatever might have made community worthwhile" (p. 92). He laments with remorse that as Rama he had sinned against Sita.

Little Mother—a goddess of ferocity, illusion, tears, food, night, beggars, savagery, and virginity—is a match for Shiva. She becomes an Untouchable, she descends countless times to earth, and she is always killed as an outlaw, in vicious acts of cruelty. In the climatic scene of the Sati-Shiva story, instead of throwing herself into Daksha's sacrificial fire, as the traditional story tells it, she is pursued, dragged, cut, and burned alive by the rapacious gods, all of whom justify themselves by claiming that she will thank them later for delivering her from her own impurity (p. 85). Her death is salvific at the conclusion of the poem because it causes the tormenting repentance of the gods and the final dissolution of time.

The only character who understands and affirms the priorities of the God of Tears and Little Mother is Slave of Time, a demon. He, like other "othered" beings classed as demons, retains some memory of compassion. "Only/slaves know the terrible results of Good" (p. 65). He sees the deadly character, the violence, of social rules.

Indeed, nearly everything in this poem is topsy-turvy. The gods are hypocritical, lascivious, cruel, indolent. They "think they are divine/and have the force of arms that can compel/others to affirm the claim as well"; they "never let themselves/live amid the slum of Earth, and Hell" (p. 52). Frenzied with desire, they battle each other and the demons for the nectar churned out of the milk-ocean at the beginning of time. They taunt Sati/Little Mother cruelly for choosing the God of Tears/Shiva as her husband and would rather tear her to pieces than allow her to marry her own choice. Even in the presence of one grieving the death of his wife—Shiva holding the burned corpse of Sati—"the gods pressed in, nudged, pointed/fingers, exclaimed, asked, burped, picked,/scratched, and ogled" (pp. 89-90). Apes and snakes are more honorable than the gods. Hell is more beautiful, for its honesty and compassion, than Heaven. And the most corrupt being of all is "Religious Man" (p. 53).

THE DEATH OF THE GODDESS

It is here that I return to the terrifying character of Hogan's brilliant reworking—"re-envisioning," as he puts it—of this ancient Hindu myth. He brings in horrifying details of the tortures and atrocities committed by humans against one another, from American slavery, the Nazi Holocaust, the Vietnam war, the Soviet "show" trials, the raw barbarity of Partition violence, and the anti-terrorism torture techniques of Islamophobic jailers. What are the weapons the gods use against one another? "Gelatinous acids that battened/on the skin/and ate the muscle, fat, and bone away/to air" (p. 36); "missiles that sprayed odorless gas" (p. 36); disgrace, shaming, and honor killing; rapes of prisoners; binding the hands of young boys and hauling them backward by the wrists to hang from trees, in front of their fathers (p. 64)…some of the examples Hogan gives are too horrible for this Introduction.

And yet, the death of the goddess, the destruction of time, of creation, of memory, bring redemption and peace. We can feel it and savor it at the conclusion to this moving poem. We experience what Hogan says about the Slave of Time, the one demon who understood. In a later life he becomes a poet who sings "pain into exquisite curls of verse./Thus from the strife of gods and the compassion of a fiend,/poetry [is] born into the mortal world" (p. 25). Hogan's devastatingly beautiful poem is an aweful gift. 🔅

—Rachel Fell McDermott
Barnard College
New York, NY

I

The Beginning of Time

༄

Before being or unbeing, truth or illusion,
before thought or the withering of experience into memory,
before duty or sin, attachment or letting go,
before all things the gods revile or protect,
before even the unsheltering void, immense, unbodied –
what is was darkness concealed in darkness only.
Then Grandfather dreamt, and the dream became
Grandfather dreaming.

First came everything that flows –
the foaming rush of waters, the ecstatic tones
of the flute, and all words, human and divine.
That was Grandmother, Moon Crescent,
Lotus Cradled, who carried in herself
All eons and orderings of time.
From Her and Him, three hundred million
gods and goddesses took form and life;
each element of dark congealed into location,
shape, dimension – uncountable genii of place.
In this first fixity, all mortal life,
all solid and all ethereal things –
what is – found unique endurance and extension.
Then, marking the outer rim of worldly order –
beyond which is vertigo of time,
baffles of thick space, and foundering chance –
a single encompassing, perfected form:
Unmoving Goddess united with the God of Dance.

II
The Origin of Grief

❧

At the start of things, gods joined in common
work and churned the frothing sea as farmers
churn the curdled milk or cream for butter.
First, came feasts of food and drink,
then herbs to ease the body and relieve the soul.
Fertility and strength, wealth and the security of home
poured forth. Abstracter qualities followed,
as warmth follows light; or satisfaction,
sacrifice: beauty of shape, hue, and motion,
knowledge of the earth, the sky, and the inconstant mind —
these too were born from the violent waves.
Then, to unify and orient each excellence of nature
and of art, duty rose, last of all,
in bodily form, exquisite in contour and in movement.
But the gods grew limitless appetites, unsatisfied
with bread and health, merit, loveliness, increase,
vigor, wisdom, bounty, belonging, obligation;
crazed with greed for unknown things, they refused
to cease at Grandfather's admonition, crying,
"You promised us immortalizing nectar.
Give!"

The God of Tears and Dance, on an icy peak,
practiced fierce asceticism to stifle appetite,
and to bring the straining mind from force to quiet
like ambient air when the wind lulls.
But the crazed demand of gods for All troubled
the slow cycle of his breathing, in and out.
Only he — of those who saw the stick

work through thick sea slush —
knew the consequences of such lust.

Darkness gathered like night on the horizon —
omnivorous time, a black tide
that carried in its virulent flood all shapes
of death, all its additions and preliminaries:
disease that eats away the throat or lung
to gasping suffocation, or corrodes the brain
to hollow-eyed perplexity and sclerosis of the mind;
the searing delirium of virus; hunger, with its first,
fanatic struggle, then gradual desuetude of will;
the bilious retching of malignancy; even
all that is now normal to the course of age —
senile decrepitude, with slow decay of recollection,
arthritic brittling of act, the thickening of sense
to dim opacity (like a clot of oily film
spread across the eye), abject dependency
of routine function, and rituals of shame
as the body grows stubbornly alien to the will.
Once, the poison cradled on the floor beneath;
now it flowed to a dark wave,
then out, from ocean, to each habitable place.
So misery assumed its first material shape.

      The gods knew what it meant;
they gasped in horror that their greed for ecstasy
had churned forth so much sorrow
from the depthless, unbeginning sea.
They scattered like unarmed crowds before an army.
"Grandfather, help us!," they pleaded. The Source of All
called to his Beloved Son, the Strangler of Demons,
the Protector of the Faith: "Throughout the three worlds,
you are known as Savior. Contain the poison.
Rescue me and all the other gods,
and all the worlds, and all created things."

But the Son too was impatient for eternity
and coveted the nectar that destroys all time;
so he refused to make the sacrifice.

The crowd, abandoned by the Savior, surged in panic,
tearing at each other's hair and clothes,
to advance themselves, to press the others back
as some buffer against the rolling tide.
Terror-struck, blood-spattered, trembling,
the manic gods crossed the flooding plain
then clambered up the shelves of frozen stone.
They stopped before the God of Tears and Anger
the Fearless One, the Source of Fire and Rain,
the Giver of Joy, God of the Left Hand,
the Conqueror of Death, the Friend. He stood
above them, balanced on one toe,
motionless, his hair swirling in bitter wind,
his arms arched high like lotus tendrils –
meditating, naked, beautiful as lotus blossoms,
nearly a mere boy to the manly gods.
They had always laughed at him before,
but now they knelt and pleaded for his help.
Only he had discipline enough
to take the venom in his throat and never swallow it
until the world dissolved to zero, until
the all-pervading Spirit, asleep, undreaming,
gathered all things back into itself –
for after that return, there is no poison
and no ambrosia, and all pain and joy
dissipate like faltering waves on traceless void.
The God of Tears pursed his lips
at their request to drain the poison from the sea.
But first his tongue, not used to bitterness, recoiled:
one drop of venom slipped into the common space
and spread like oil across the surface,
tainting all that lives with stains of time.

THE DEATH OF THE GODDESS

The big shots ground their teeth with rage
and retreated to the churning place again.
As his neck stained blue with seeping poison
the Friend cursed the thankless crowd,
never, until the final end of time,
to find that ecstasy
all beings wish to find.

But he soon repented what he'd said.
He crossed the weedy plain, its long grass
still trampled down along erratic paths
where gods ran through, like squealing pigs
who'd seen the farmer with the mallet, and the queer look.
A dozen cliffs, the rock still stained
from the black surge, shouldered out into the sea.
The Giver of Joy, the God of Tears stood
at the edge of heaven's cleft. Below him, dizzy
with fatigue, a hundred fifty million gods,
toiled at the churning stick, pursuing bliss.
Their arms ached from the strain, their muscles tore,
their legs gave way; one by one
they fell, mere ruined forms, down
into the white foam of the lapping sea.
Some moaned inconsolable despair.
Others urged one final try—
these, spitting out the sand, dragged
their bodies up from seawrack, bound like ships
in thick weed, blinded by the sun which seemed
hotter every moment and unsetting. Most
collapsed along the path, few reached the line
of pull. They tried to speed or at least sustain
the turn and grind. But now the sea
fell to dull quiet; the limp cord
slipped between their blistered hands, trailed
faint eddies along the sands and out,
to universal axis, from the surf and shore.

That day, many gods wept
beside the sea, cursing fate, cursing
the one drop of death that spread pain
throughout three worlds, cursing the Source
of Tears and Anger – Lefty, Oddball,
Friend of Outcastes, Consoler of the Enemy –
though he was the one who saved them from the flood.
That day, the three worlds were filled
with keening cries and accusations of the gods.

The Friend thought, "Here, too, desire is pain."
And yet, as if there were no consequences –
for himself, for them, for all who move
and feel in disordered spaces of brute things –
he whispered "Nectar," and the golden liquid, thick
as honey, sprayed high into the vault of air.
It held there for a moment, glimmering like
stars before the sky's blue dome,
then fell like rain against the land, dried
to tables of bare salt, irregular and white,
within a receding line of desiccated bush.
It drenched the fallen gods as well – and they
revived, as vigorous, self-certain, and resolute
as at the time, already ancient, of their birth
from the union of the sky and watery earth.

III
Paradise Lost

࣫

For weeks the gods had hardly waded to the land;
Any thought of love, wealth, or duty
faded, ideas of liberation withered
like unplucked fruit after a drought
dries up the roots; one goal
drove their crazed labors on
to equivocal ends, one lust sustained them
as their bodies wore away (like legendary mendicants,
ingesting only air for a thousand years):
to round their sunken guts and plump their hams
with nectar (as grandma fattens up her son's
or daughter's scrawny child with cookies and with pies).
That image spurred the gods to split their joints
in unprogressing struggle against chaos and uncertainty,
as the dream of a cowherd god goads
virgin milkmaids to the sacred and erotic dance,
or the disembodied notion of all-embracing
Void drives monks to seek the absolute
still point and the ecstasies of trance.

But the wives were unconvinced their boys had brains enough
to labor out success from such a doubtful start.
Each goddess questioned the ability of men
to turn vain toil to profit – and lead them,
in the end, to realms of deathless, unimaginable bliss.
The utter sameness through a drag of time
without result – except decline of vigor
and erosion of the drive – seemed to confirm their doubts.
So, fuming with contempt, and suffering

the strain of sexual neglect, the goddesses
retreated from the plain, like hermits into wilderness,
and abandoned their emasculated mates,
to what delusions they might later fabricate
for propping up a failed sense of self.
Never, in all worlds, in any age,
was there such exodus of beauty
from a single place, for each divinity,
though different from all others, was flawless in her kind,
exhausting all perfections of that one form,
as the idea of a circle exhausts the thing itself,
without impinging on the purity of any other
geometric shape. So the shores,
once filled with milling crowds, with talk,
with laughter, with the heavy smells of food and subtler
scents of incense or perfume, now became
a bare, quiet shelf above the water
and above the foolish, struggling men. Now
the wind passed over empty space,
stirring an ephemeral whirl, here and there,
of white fine dust, like funeral ashes
scattered on a sacred river by the wandering air.

   The gods, fixated on the one, fantastic thing,
and on the quest, didn't seem to see, or care,
that all their wives had left behind the ring
of bay that once had compassed their shared life.
But now they felt the healing drops of nectar
fill them with the urge and memory of love.
Now, they recalled their lives along the shore,
and cursed themselves, that this obsession forced
their wives to leave what might have been a home—
and cursed again that at the time, they made
no sign of protest, of promise, or remorse.

Only the Savior, the Dear Son, foresaw
this strife between the tongue and heart, or the belly
and the groin – for he, like the Friend, understood
desire. The others staggered in conflicting drives.
First, they set their face into the wind,
flailing against the tide, and tried to reach
the heavenly swill. But, once they started out,
they wavered, then turned back, retreating.
With equal frenzy, taking awkward steps
through waves that raised them from the floor, they tried –
without success – to push against the sand
or swim to shore, now aiming for the woods
where they imagined gentle and repentant wives,
their hands and lips and soft triangles of rough
impatient for the solid thicknesses of love.

While the ordinary rank of gods stood dazed
by alternating greed and lust, the Son
took on a woman's form and seemed to each of them
the idol of his private want. To one,
he was dark-skinned and proud; to another, pale
and demure; to a first group, fat as butter;
to a second, thin as straw; to these, his face
was long and sad, an appeal for tenderness;
to those, it was round as a full moon
and jolly as the New Beer Fest; with some,
he wore transparent muslin of dancing girls;
for others, he put on the cloth of servants,
coarsely spun and prickly to the touch. Thus
all 150 million gods,
entranced by insubstantial fictions shaped
in dreaming minds from lust and fancy, faced
in finite and particular form, the principle
that spurs, sustains, and in the end destroys
every belief: Illusion, the primal drive
that makes all seeming matter out of void.

THE DEATH OF THE GODDESS

The gods could not resist the vision that arose
before them on the glimmering surfaces of sea.
Each one, groaning, sore with need,
tore at his garments with one hand and with
the other reached to grab the airy nothing
that he mistook for a goddess' flesh. But when
this vision raised her palm and paused, they waited.
The Savior, in his 150 million forms,
locked back the jaws above each
spring, balancing the bait within.
"I have watched you all these days,
admiring what you do and feeling for you
the way a woman feels toward a man.
I saw your wife abandon you, like all the others–
She mocked your work, your manhood, your goals and hopes.
How foolish those old crones seem now!
But I always knew that you'd succeed.
I never had a single doubt that you could draw
the pure idea from a murky thing. Take me,
my love, crush me in your strong arms,
pierce me with your organ, thick and hard
as stone phalloi worshiped by barren women.
Take me here on the soft sand
beside the lapping water or there, on ground
that's firm, unmoving, with soft grass below
the arching curve of back and knees, a perfect
place for love. But let me gather up
and store your portion of the nectar first
in this gold urn. You wouldn't want
to lose what's yours in a rash act.
I'll hide it there, beyond the fallen axle,
past the salt bank, in the long grass.
Before returning, I'll scoop my finger in the pot,
Then smear my tongue with honey of eternal bliss,
So you, my lord, will taste
Ambrosia every time we kiss."

Deranged with lust, the men agreed to the request,
blind to any consequence. And so
each god, from ignorance and vertigo
surrendered to the beguiling Ally all
his private share of joy. Then our Absolute Protector
gathered the ambrosia into one fat pot,
placed it on his head, and waded to the shore; he swayed
lithe hips in sensuous, slow waves
as he passed up from milky water onto land.
The muslin of his skirt clung to rounded flesh,
and turned translucent from the water and the brilliant sun.
The gods stared open-mouthed, their organs
throbbing hotly. When he reached the shore,
and set down his load on the dry ground,
he turned back and peeled off the dress,
revealing his ordinary self. Two
or three of the gaping gods opened their lips
in disbelief to say the Savior's name
as he and all the nectar disappeared,
rising through the sky and fiery air.
The rest stood paralyzed, astonished, and ashamed.

Breaking free, after a while, from stupor,
the stirring mass of hoodwinked gods
blamed one another for the loss,
fought – and wept in wild, sobbing cries,
like teething infants, for the vanished drink,
sweet as breastmilk to a hungry child.

IV
An Act of Compassion

&

So war began from this first lack—
the gush that fixed their hopes, then
the baffled flow and theft, the blank gap
where, sun-like, ore had flowed.
But it was a queer, incoherent war.
There were no sides, no generals or chiefs,
no ordered strategies that usually guide
a conflict to resolution through victory
or mutual accord. Most simply struck
whoever was at hand. Sometimes, they first attacked
with words, rude gestures, and with spit.
Arms followed—a splinter of the churning stick,
a shard of urn, pink rocks of coral,
or, if nothing else, then nails and teeth,
something that would tear the skin, and hurt.
The blood of so many gods seeped
into the pale sea, darkening the tide.
Here and there, a pair of cooler heads
joined to make and desecrate effigies
of Our Protector, but they soon fell
to mutual blame as well, and the icons lay
along the shore, unbattered, restful,
with mocking smiles. Now and then, some tried
to take up the rod and churn again.
They hoped that greater force would find and cut
another vein of nectar. The churning grew
furious, but drew out nothing new;
at last, the laborers collapsed into the tide,
drank brine, not ambrosia, floundered,

half-drowned, against the swelling waves
that crashed and shivered in the sound. A few misfits
saw that their own sins had led
to this consuming fear and mutual hate.
Instead of bludgeoning imaginary
foes, they cursed, and whipped themselves in slow
processions, fell on their knees, tore off
their royal clothes, cried out for more
and greater suffering, and beat their heads
against the rocky strand. The blood dried
on their faces, on their hands, and in their matted hair
and stained the barren, salt-white shore.

    The demons howled around the violent place,
exultant as they viewed confusion and despair engulf
this self-imagined master race.
Flesh-Eaters scooped up blood
by handfuls from pools in which the gods collapsed,
and savored the metallic taste as if it were sweet wine.
The liquor trickled down the corners of their mouths,
staining their neck and shoulders and their chest with fine,
sanguinary lines; the breasts of Demonesses too
were streaked and patched with reddish black, like idols
who have tasted lungs or beating hearts in sacrifice.
Intoxicated with the drink, they sang cacophonous tunes
off-key, and danced erratic paths
along the surf. But one—his name meant
"Slave of Time"—went up the sliding dunes
that arced the inlet, crossed the salt flats,
passed through the prickly brush into the woods
and sudden darkness, as if he stepped from day to night,
into the pulsing cries of the macaques, the ceaseless hisses
of the serpents—two nations driven from their homes
by the expansive gods. Handicapped by laws of war,
they would not slit the throats of enemies
sleeping in their tents, kill children, bind

the hands of captives, then grind their brains
into the rock with clubs. Their soldiers
were not spurred to heights of valor
by the thought that they could rape Barbarian wives
just after murdering the husbands before their eyes.
The gods, whose every act is duty, followed
no such rules, and quickly won.
One million Monkeys, and five times
that number of the Serpents fled divine assault,
sought refuge deep in the uncultivated dark,
and hoped that gods, knowing of no further
benefit to the fight, would halt from their pursuit at the perimeter
of night. Arriving at asylum, the apes and snakes
embraced peripatetic lives, homeless,
wandering unadorned, eating just
what fell unplucked along the path.
The place that was once their land – thick
groves of fruit- and flower-bearing trees –
became the salty space before the shore,
one broad band of forest felled
to spread out camps, to fuel fires
of sacrifice, to form the second churning stick
that dredged up ecstasy, and strife.

Having passed beyond the border into wild,
Slave of Time, like a hunter or a sporting
king, followed out the tracks of wandering
deer; they sought clear water,
while he sought to bring peace back
to an implacable thing. For a fortnight
he pressed on without rest, and seemed
to have achieved no forward progress.
Each path he passed appeared identical
with those he passed before, and he began to wonder
if he was tracing out a single round,
trapped unknowingly within a narrow compass,

like a fly that circles the same flame,
until it collapses in a crumpled heap
beside the wick. He had almost fallen into despair,
and turned to find his way back to the shore,
when suddenly he surfaced from the dark
into a blinding brilliancy of clear,
shimmering water, and luminous air.

Once his eyes adjusted to the light, he saw
the pond where Grandfather – Immensity, Eternal Home,
Shaper of Life and Death – reclined on a bed
of roses; and Grandmother – Goddess of Rivers,
Giver of Speech, Source of Knowledge – played
her flute that was the origin of every sound.
The monkeys' pulsing shrieks, the sibilant wheeze
of snakes, had faded now and the entire place
was silent, except for that one goddess' tune.
The emotion of the piece was grief, and all creation
seemed to feel the sadness of the thing, and of the common,
personal, lingering life, whose traces it sustained
in each listener's memory and now-remembering
mind. Lions curled at the goddess' feet;
from the trees, turtledoves cooed
their fluttering cries; does stood motionless,
jaws drooping, eyes watery and wide;
but most pathetic of all the unwild beasts
gathered in that peaceful space of first retreat,
were the beautiful, ungainly elephants who
dropped awkwardly onto their knees,
then collapsed upon the ground as if
wounded by a spear that pierced into a fatal place,
and dug their brows against the earth.
Grandfather too was pained, and when she stopped,
he took the instrument from Grandmother's hand,
to rest his head upon her breast,
and dry his eyes in wave-like pleats of dress.

Then Grandmother saw the visitor
and called to him, saying: "Respected Slave of Time,
what has brought you from the churning sea
to join our peaceful hermitage?"
"Most admirable goddess, your music was so
entrancing that I almost forgot my goal
in traveling to this place where no devil is allowed.
I have come to ask for your protection of the gods."
Grandfather sat upright, wary of a fiend
who seemed to sacrifice his private gain for "Right."
Slave of Time explained, "Your favorite son
deceived the other gods. He shaped himself
into a replica of their desire
and they gave everything away they strove
so hard to draw up from the mire,
exchanging it for promises – of love."

A smile broke out on Grandfather's lips;
joy suffused his face at the mention of this
beloved boy; he rocked in stifled laughter
on the bank, delighted at his son's mischievous
pranks and the muddle of the other gods.
For of all deities and all created things,
he loved this last-born child most.
He recalled the thrill of gathering up the tiny,
trembling limbs into his arms, holding
the baby's ear against his heart, so he would hear
that soothing rhythm of the blood; remembered
too the festive babble of the precious youth,
the rubbery swagger of his first walk,
the wide-eyed wonder at such simple things
as the designs sketched out along a wall with chalk,
the fluttering colors of butterflies above the lawn,
the insubstantial surface of a reflecting pond.
When Grandfather thought of our Compatriot,

the Savior, Right Arm of Faith—though now
he was a manly god with a wife and many palaces,
authority, vast wealth, a train of slaves—
he always saw a diapered infant,
who mashed his food into his hair and toes
and gurgled laughter as he surveyed the mess he'd made.
Once, as Grandmother thought to reprimand
the misbehaved little imp, he pointed
to the slop spread out across the floor,
shook his small head, and with
a dour frown of censure, and a contracted brow,
he scolded Grandfather, source of all: "You
naughty Papa!," he said, then giggled
once again and toddled out into the yard,
trailing crushed banana, rice, and curd.

After a pause, puzzled by Grandfather's glee,
Slave of Time elaborated on his account:
"First, the lesser gods cried out
in longing, anger, and despair. After this,
they blamed each other for the loss. Threats followed.
Then attacks, against whoever was around—
not from hate so much as fear,
like cornered rats, vaguely aware
that the law of war was 'Thou shalt kill
or else be killed.' I traveled here,
hoping you, Grandfather, could
re-order chaos, calm their panic
into peace—or at least negotiate
a truce, then, like a healer or a priest,
with pills or prayers, potions or quarantines,
end this epidemic of inflicting pain,
doctor the mad gods, and make them sane."

For this one insubordination,
the demon was condemned to live a thousand spans

of human time. In his first birth, despite
the blank forgetfulness of men and women
that erases from the mind all trace of good
that they have learned in former lives,
he still was able to recall the scene beside
the lotus pond, and Grandmother's sound.
From this, to the astonishment of all around
he sang pain into exquisite curls of verse.
Thus from the strife of gods and the compassion of a fiend,
poetry was born into the mortal world.

V
Illusion Regained

࿔

Having rewarded, in the usual way, the slave
who carried news unflattering to the master race,
Grandfather retraced the demon's path, returning
from serene retreat into the seething world.
But when he descended to the sea, it was a desolate place.
The gods were everywhere, but nowhere, like the frail shades
of ancestors at a funeral or a sacrificial feast.
He looked around. He called to them.
Nauseous, paranoid, broken and confused
they had cowered behind rocks, squeezed into crevices
along the cliffs, sunk beneath the sea or dug
into the strand (their mouths just visible
if you knew where to look, above the water and the sand),
desperate for an end to the horror they began.
Hearing Grandfather's call, they stumbled out,
singly or in small bands, from where they hid,
pale with terror, their eyes red
from tears and sea-salt; violent tremors
shook their hands; their legs could barely
stand their battered frames upright;
their breath was strained and shuddering, like
the baffled inhalation of a frightened, crying child.
As they reached the rising dunes, on which Grandfather stood,
they fell onto the ground, pleaded with him, and accused.
Some cried out for justice or revenge;
others begged him for reversion, mere return
to a time when they had never heard of nectar.
But, punctuating all particular demands
and giving them an organizing aim—as when

the tonic makes all other notes into a theme—
was one, recurring, piteous refrain:
"Grandfather, restore us—heal the pain."

The Shaper then dispatched horse-bodied twins,
messengers of gods, bearers of the dawn,
to call Demon-Strangler down from Paradise,
to bring the drink for which all beings longed.
But he already knew the outcome of the case—
no god would ever taste the nectar
in this perfected state, and, in the end,
the churning of the sea would yield only poison.

When Demon Strangler alighted at the water's edge,
Grandfather ordered him to give up the stash.
The savior whined that all the other gods
had willingly passed their cut of spoils to him.
"I did not," Grandfather replied.
"And, in the final count, whatever properties
they hold—houses, land, jewels, gold,
cattle, ships, wagons, handcrafted goods,
and all the multiple wealth of sea and earth—
belong to me alone. So, my dearest
child, return the nectar that is mine."
Hearing this, Protector of the Faith gave up
the sauce that woozy gods had poured into his pot.
But the Shaper of Life and Death did not divide
the stuff into 150 million parts.
"There is no point in drinking nectar now,"
he said. "We are living in the best of times.
From here, all change is a decline.
Today, gods and goddesses, men and women,
are stronger, kinder, and more virtuous in thought
and deed than they will ever be again.
No god can die in this first
period of time, in the next, nor in the third,

and none can suffer from enduring pain. Today,
no loss is irretrievable, no
agony is unredeemed. To drink the nectar
now would waste its best effect.
In this age, there's no lasting harm
from which it could protect a god. Indeed,
look for yourselves, the injuries you suffered
just an hour ago are healed, gone
from open sores to scabs, from scabs to scars,
and from scars back to unblemished skin."
It was true. They realized that, since the resolution
of the war, their pain had gradually ceased, as if
the nectar had been released a second time
and they were drenched again in healing rain.

"But other epochs will succeed this perfect era.
First will come the age of ignorance
named for demons. Then the age of beasts,
ruled by brute drives. Then, last
and most depraved, the age of humans, when
compassion has withered like an unused limb,
and nowhere in the three worlds will anyone
recall the practice or the aim of duty.
In that age, even the most just
women, the most moral men, will give
consent to those who harm the innocent –
and most will actively advance the violent act;
for no one in that time can live
without both suffering and inflicting pain.
It is only in that Age of Universal Cruelty
that even gods require nectar to survive.
I will, therefore, conceal the ambrosia until
the evil of that final age is ripe.
Then, at a festival for all the gods,
or almost all, and all the goddesses, I will

pour out the nectar into cups and bowls
so everyone can down what he or she deserves.
Some of you might then recall
how, even in the age of innocence,
you were all willing to lay waste
the heavenly world for one more taste
of juice, and love from an imaginary girl."

Grandfather had first planned a harder reprimand,
spelling out in graphic scenes the consequences
of their fantastical dreams and violence.
But his anger melted to compassion when he looked across
the shamed and hopeful faces of the gaping gods.
For he knew well that, in the final age,
the nectar declines too. It cannot give
the drinker an eternal life, or endless bliss.
He knew also what the feast would be,
and what tragedy would mark the end of ages:
the death of the goddess. Yes, that he remembered.
Indeed, he thought, the violence of this final history
could, in the end, make gods renounce the nectar
and seek, instead, the poisonous tide, for in the time
of universal and deliberate pain, the greatest misery
would be to think one could not die.

VI
The Birth of the Goddess

❧

Spring came, and with that first thaw,
the Ethereal Goddess – Virgin-Girl, Savage,
Little Beauty, Fierce Nature, Sacrifice,
Food-Giver, Goddess of Tears, Mother
of All – took on again her fluid form.
She was the frozen lakes, the snow, now
melted into flux: first, slow drops
and trickles of pale blue, carving erratic
paths through caves of ice, then runnels
no broader than a woman's hand
and clear as air; they grew
to glittering, soft streams, their muffled rush
the goddess' whisper murmuring beneath
the shrieks of wind that, from the onset of the dream,
had pierced the air like widows keening.
For a certain space, the brook appeared to sink
beneath the hard, hoary, crusted earth,
or just to end. Then, suddenly, the white,
unyielding surface of a broad expanse, that seemed
to bear all weight as solid land,
cracked to jagged floes that split again
to many shards, when hurled against the rocks
by the growing violence of waves. Then,
tumbling unexpectedly across the threshold
of its firm bed, the river plunged headlong
into the wisps of air and mere blank space
that stretched between the divine and human place.

THE DEATH OF THE GODDESS

Before this, there was no flowing water
on the earth, to parallel the ocean of the gods;
there were no seas to isolate and link
the different lands, no rivers to bear commerce
between towns, no lakes that would sustain
a settled life for those who live and die
many times in Grandfather's one day
and night. After that first fall, the river
spread throughout the mortal world, flowing
into countless channels that would in time
speed conquest, plunder, and the exercise of will
by the few who hold the greatest stores of gold
and who wield the sharpest, hardest spears and swords.
But, after these mere secular streams
drained whatever was profane from the heavenly source,
a gathering fall of pristine rain reshaped
the newborn goddess into one final form—
the end toward which each mortal body strives:
beloved Ganga, who carries in her cradling arms,
to final rest, all that remains of human lives.

Immersion in the clustering waves, the cool,
thick tumble and bright spray, smooth
and heavy on the skin—water which was
the Goddess's soft weight and yielding flesh,
now released from boundaries of fixed shape
and place: This was the Friend's first taste
of ecstasy, for until then he had refrained
from all corporeal joy as slavery of the mind.
This engulfment carried in its train as well
intimations of the culminating bliss,
the ultimate release from self—could
that, he wondered, too be union?
Looking up into the brilliant blue
dome of sky and diffuse light, through
the sheer glimmering mirror of the waterfall,

he saw—no more distant than the reach
of their own arms to touch, fingers and palms—
the perfection and the prototype of form, more
exquisite than any fancy taken on
by the Savior to confuse the gullible gods; and yet
she was substantial as the Lord of Tears himself.
It was as if the first idea, the first shape
that oriented thought and drive, had taken on
perception, intent, and act. He was transfixed,
and blank to place, or time, or flux of sense—
like a dervish or a nectar addict, fallen into trance.

    "Does she speak? Speak, Goddess.
Does she feel the cool and heat,
recognize the face she sees,
feel love and hate, sorrow, mercy,
all the affections that modify the will, and bruise
one's peace, share the private now
fading endlessly into remembrance
and fixless sense of unreachable, ephemeral I?
Or is she Illusion only, just a trick
of flickering light and shadow played by blood
and memory on unsteady sight?"
Her skin was blinding in its glimmering brightness and so
like the mountain snow, he almost thought
it melted at the waist and flowed into the river
where he tried to stand. But her hair
was black as moonless night, or as the poison
he still held inside his throat,
and her mouth was red as berries or fresh blood.
Suddenly he knew who waded toward him
in the swelling pool, and as once he granted
other gods their one desire, now
he named his own, not "Nectar," but what
is still more rare and beautiful, and yet
accessible to all the sentient forms, no matter

what their rank, their station, or their place in law.
He whispered it, with trembling lips, in awe.

But he was the Top Dog of Ascetics,
Champion in Thirst, Icon of Hunger,
Emblem of Chastity. Above everything
he sought and most admired discipline of mind.
As a result, he shunned the only soul
he ever did or would desire, and withdrew
from the caresses of the heavenly spring, climbed
the cliffs again, in biting wind, to immerse
himself instead in the mere emptiness of things
and in bodily trials that, he hoped, would end
the self through self-denial.

Before the moment she was borne up
by foaming water to a ledge of rock
above the heavenly plains, the Goddess of Tears
saw nothing; she didn't see Joy-Giver's face,
hear his voice, or watch him leave. First
of all material things, Our Little Girl
spied the society of gods — drunken, lecherous, swaggering.
She witnessed the company of men and women too,
pale imitation of the gods — pride lacking
excellence, inebriation without joy, lechery
and violence with no limit drawn by duty,
by understanding, or even by a brute
sense of kinship, a recognition of shared
parentage, the common, ancestral root.

Word soon spread among the gods
that here was some fresh meat ready
for a taste. They crowded to the plain
and eyed her parts. Divine flesh
unpossessed, and thus unsoiled by intimate
acquaintance and slow spite of married life:

the mere idea made them feverish with desire
to plunge into the cooling stream, and drink.
In time, a few of the more forward gods
shook off the gape-mouthed, swooning
languor of their excess heat, and set out
to woo the new-born goddess; so,
they primped below the polished silver plates
and above the still, reflective pools, to compete
in her obligatory choice of a mate:
first, they liberally doused their skulls
with peanut oil and perfume, plumped up
their shining curls with fine-tined combs,
applied thick strokes of blue-black
kohl around the eyes, used sandal paste to stain
their broad, hard chests and rippling fronts,
slipped into necklaces strung with coral and small
shells, pinned on their pendant earrings
of black pearl, and twined diamond-clustered
bands around their manly arms. At last,
when they had tied the hip-knots in their best
sarongs, they sauntered toward the shore
with glittering gifts and honeyed tongues.

　　Soon the far bank of the little brook
was lined with rows of supplicants. The highest
ranking of the lot brought irreplicable prizes
thieved from the common churning of the sea: chariots
thickly laid with gold and precious stones,
drawn by fiery horses, swift and brilliant
as rays of the sun; granite-bodied men
and delicate boys to cater to her every whim;
slaves waiting to perform whatever she'd command;
vast armies for domination and defense;
balms and medicines to end the sense of pain;
mushrooms and moonshine, that drive the mind
to flights of vibrant and fantastic ecstasy.

THE DEATH OF THE GODDESS

When she refused these bribes, the gods
re-shaped the gold into her likeness,
fell prostrate at the statue's feet, and prayed;
for days, they poured their offerings in holy fires
and stained the idol with blood sacrifice;
they even slit the throats of boys and girls,
since there was no on-going war
to boast their toughness and ability to kill.
Recoiling in horror at their acts, the Goddess of Tears
repudiated their pursuit more vehemently still.

Angry and baffled, the gods regrouped,
passed through the stream, then pressed
close around her with malicious looks.
They called together armies for support.
When summoned, they appeared from all the regions
—from heaven, from the earth, and hell.
The last were the most vicious and most stupid
devils that the gods could find, paid goons
who sold their services to the one eternal enemy
of all their kind; every day,
for a weekly packet of small beer,
they disemboweled a dozen of their dear kin—
though, as a bonus for their loyal use of might,
they took home, every night, their victims'
paltry stock of wealth, too meager for divinities
to care. So, the field grew crowded
with military gods and armies of the damned. All
this vast and threatening show of force was called
by the resentful gods to brutalize and overrule
the will of a mere wispy slip of girl.

Little Beauty, Peace of the Night, Goddess
of Tears looked past the pressing crowd of gods
to the army of one-hundred-headed djinns.
Their eyes flashed wildly, red with drink;

their teeth, tapering to fine points, were pocked
with clots of meat scavenged from the sacrificial place;
their hands each clutched a sword, a mace,
a spear, some instrument, not only to destroy,
or to bring death, but to shape the proper kind
of visible pain so it extends compulsion,
winning more civilians' hearts and minds:

Arrows with filled tips that spread fine
needles when they pierced the flesh, to slice
again the inner parts each time
the victim touched the wound in pain.

Gelatinous acids that battened on the skin
and ate the muscle, fat, and bone away
to air. Children plunged in nearby streams;
women pulled buckets from the village wells;
men fell, despite the stink and film,
into malarial pools, that stained the fields.
They tried to wash away the godly paste
that, in an hour or two, would chew
the wrist off from the hand, or burrow through
the breast-bone to the lung, or skull into the brain,
and leave behind the smell of burning hair;
but no amount of water would flush out
the rot of heavenly stuff from spreading sores.
As the agony increased, the victims shrieked
and wept like lunatics, and flailed against the sand,
as if they had caught fire and could suffocate
the flames. In time, the frenzy lulled to stray
spasms of the corroded trunk and puppet limbs,
which lessened, in frequency and force, then ceased,
at last, in death, the long-desired release.

Missiles that sprayed odorless gas throughout
the enemy town. First, the victims felt

nothing, then a trembling of the head and hands,
erratic flutters of the heart and tightness in the chest,
then aimless fear as, over time, a palsy,
increasingly severe, suffused their frame.
When the clouds of gas passed through
and dissipated across the neighboring farms —
though no one knew at first —
they left just colorless sketches
and strange memories, alarming and fantastic,
of the vigorous, normal life that went before —
the life of daily dressing, meals, work,
walking through the street, milling about a shop,
the routine hours passed each day,
the festive nights that ended ceremonial weeks.
All this bright and dour tragi-comedy
with its tedious and touching schemes,
its pettiness, its stupid and endearing dreams
its resentful disappointments and silly loves
had passed away with the poisoned air,
to be replaced by the pathetic, private theatre
of individuals, in pain, alone.
If they realized in time, before the trembling grew
too violent for them to hold a knife
and slice their wrists, they made a quicker end of it.
But those who let the crucial moment pass,
Lingered on for days, or even weeks,
undying and with no relief;
for only gods can buy and sell the medicine
and skill that soothe the wounded parts or calm
the hearts of dying children, women, men.

    Weapons of illusion too were beaten out
in the godly forges. One tactic was disgrace,
where innocent men or women are reviled
for heinous crimes throughout the state —
tried in closed chambers, or in a public show

denied by a pageant of repenting partisans.
Spurned by one's husband or one's wife
for false proofs of lechery and general vice;
reviled by one's comrades for fraud, extortion, graft;
denounced by one's parents or one's child
for unnamable evils of intent and act,
their sobbing voices drenched with shame for ties
of birth they wish they could retract.
Sometimes, replies to calumny are stifled with the threat:
"If your lips open to refuse the slightest
of these truths–established by a tribunal of the gods,
for furtherance of duty and to preserve the common good–
your spouse, your youngest child, your mother too,
may wish that they had never seen
the light of day. I believe that you have heard
of poison gas, and its effects upon the nerves."

These and other weapons were stored up
in the heavenly arsenals that Little Beauty saw.
Thus the most innocent of deities
and the last born, was disallowed the soothing fancy
of benevolence and Universal Right
from which we each began our ordinary span of life.

The gods leered at the frail, bewildered goddess,
pressed forward more, and growled about
her generation's ignorant indifference to tradition and its laws.
"You have almost reached … the woman's age";
"By summer, your fertile time will start";
"All society will be blood-stained if you violate
established custom and remain alone for long."
As if it lingered in her mind from a prior life,
the Mother of All recalled this rite, and replied
"So, this is the day set for my engagement, and you
are all competing for my hand. But I forget–
just what am I supposed to do?"

THE DEATH OF THE GODDESS

Almost in a single voice, they cried,
"Choose." "And you will not dispute my pick?"
"No," they replied, but now their words were disaligned,
and the answer was not a chorus, but a grating noise
of syllables, unsynchronized, hard to hear
and understand. Then, the crowd of gods
that had formed itself into one thing,
like lumps of molten gold gathered in
a single, shaping cast, began to crack
apart, just as molded metal forms
that have been wrongly poured or cooled
fissure along the lines of stress.
Some jostled for advantage, to draw their face,
shape, or wealth into the goddess' line of sight;
others, on the fields, sought to display their skills
in horsemanship, archery, or some rough sport.
But even brief rivalry breeds hate;
now, it grew from a private sentiment
to unambiguous dispute: verbal abuse,
shoves, scuffles, here and there a cut,
a torn robe, a bruise. But demon armies
banded at the limits, silent, massive, waiting.
Their sight dissuaded gods from breaking out
again in internecine war that day,
For none of them is so insane to trust
a loyalty sustained by trifling pay.

Undaunted by the threatening horde,
disgusted by the thought of marriage to a noble thug,
the Goddess of Tears, Food-Giver, Illusion's
Foe stared out across the plains,
the waters and the mountains, wondering, disheartened.
Beyond the far phalanx and their spears, like snarling
teeth around the angry gods, she saw
waves of gazelles leaping in tall grass,
a clutter of water buffalo, motionless as idols

or meditating saints, scattered through
the shallow brook close by the source —
their skins shimmered in red sun.
Above this scene, between the crags of stone,
here and there a clutch of prickly weeds
had broken through; she watched the bleating goats,
staggered at odd intervals across the slope,
balance their queer shapes implausibly
on spiky knobs and in small hollows of the rock
to tear up stray clumps of stuff,
chew the fibrous halms with slow-moving
jaws. Perched on their precarious heights,
they gazed out, through disdainful eyes,
on all things good and evil,
demonic and divine. Little Beauty smiled at the haughty,
harmless glare of mountain goats and remembered,
from before her birth, the gentle, tearful stares
of cows, uncheered even with the garlands
strung around their necks by loving farmers;
the eyes of dogs that have been kicked too much,
filled like those of demons, with pathetic hope;
the watchful eyes of langurs before a garden
gate, as they communicate through simple cries where
the farmer is and if he is a threat to those inside,
munching on flowers pulled off the vines;
and the eyes of predators, so like
the eyes of men, which, along the course
of the pursuit and kill, show fury, dread,
forgetfulness, fat satisfaction, but not remorse.

Then, she saw a being similar to gods
in form, but odd in habit and bearing, as if
he had been raised by strangers in a foreign place,
practicing obscure customs and alien rites.
He sat alone, naked and unkempt, in meditation
on a shelf of stone, high in the distant range,

just at the point where the drops of melted ice
first joined into a trickling flow,
the start of what, below, became the river
of the heavens, then, reaching to the end
of its celestial course, filled up
the dry oceanbeds of earth. There,
at the sacred source, a pale, scrawny kid,
with a band of bluish black around the neck,
chanted in slow, reverberating tones, the first
articulate sound, sung by Grandmother
at her birth. A motley pack of brutes
lounged around the ledge. A leopard slept
and purred soft syllables in dreams.
A serpent gently licked his hand, rubbed
a jaw against his hair, and curled into an "O"
around his shoulders, like a sacred amulet.
A panther lapped up spill from pockets
by the baby stream, and played, as if
she were a kitten, small as children's hands,
who trips into a saucer filled with milk,
screws up her spattered nose and shakes
her face to spray away the tickling drops.
Looking at the air that swirled about the place,
the goddess could not say if what she saw
was lotus petals or ashes of the dead that fell
like snow onto that small and puzzling space.

  She was unsure of who or what this crazy
mendicant with his incongruous array
of beasts might be, and yet it seemed
that, as she looked at this sinewy string
of a wild boy whom she had never met,
or even seen, that, in another age,
she loved him and had been
loved, worked toward common aims,
shared thoughts and acts with him as friends,

till some forgotten, painful, and unnecessary end.

As she continued to ignore their pleas,
the gods grew even more belligerent.
They pressed against her, jostling on all sides,
with their hot breath and oily skin. Then
they began to bellow that she had better name
her choice before the consequences became—
but here they couldn't think of how to end.
They clenched their fists. Their cheeks turned radish-red.
They worked their lips in queer, comic ways,
without finding a single word to say.
Finally, one tongue-tied boob
gave up on finding just the proper
phrase, and barked instead the following threat:
"Perhaps you would prefer to service
150 million grooms
between now and this afternoon." She thought
she could reply to this adolescent posturing,
"From what I've seen of things,
that would be short work, indeed."
But she didn't care enough to mock them.
Instead, she pointed—beyond the stream, beyond
the demon armies, beyond the plain, high
into the distant, ash-white peaks—
"I take him," she said, and walked
out from the encircling, now-ousted crowd
of astounded suitors toward her chosen spouse.

For a moment, everything was silent and the gods
strained to see some speck of starvling
on a distant ledge. Then, suddenly, one god
at the far edge of the craning crowd recognized
the notorious pariah god and cried,
"It's Oddball!" "You can't be serious—
of 150 million gods, she chose

The Smelly Clod?" "It's Pretzel Legs she wants?"
The gods turned to face each other,
thunderstruck and astonished at the news,
their mouths curved downward in distressful frowns.
But at the very moment their eyes met,
heaving bellylaughs wracked their divine frames,
like convulsions caused by sickness of the brain.
Once, this withered to giggles and stray sighs,
but when the gods looked up and saw
each other's faces for a second time,
honking guffaws broke out again like farts.
Overcome, their knees turned rubbery
and deities collapsed to helpless, rolling lumps
along the sodden ground. Massive warriors,
thick-necked, stone-bottomed, rippling,
lay senseless and immobilized by glee;
tears flowing from their eyes, they tossed about
in sand and stream, kicked backwards
with both feet, high against the air,
like some queer, snorting ass,
stuck on its back. Between the spurts
of merriment, they wheezed, "She hurts to think about
My-Little-Dollop-of-Ingudi-Oil?,"
"She wants a taste of Count-My-Bones?,"
"Oh, the cramps are killing me," and clenched
their aching bellies or their cheeks,
their bodies wrenched in suffocating spasms of hilarity.
Others were driven to incontinence, and soiled
their silk sarongs – "She lusts on His Holiness
All-Wealth-Is-Pain?" "Teacher
of All Teachers, whose very name means
'My-Loincloth-Is-Made-From-The-Bark-Of-Trees'–
that's his first name, and the last:
'You-Know-Right-Diet-Can-Blunt-The-Lusts'–
now there you have a young girl's dream!"
"Exalted Mahatma, renowned throughout three

worlds as 'Promise-Her-Anything-But-
Give-Her-Uncooked-Leaves-And-Nuts,'
as material for a husband, he can't be topped!"
"Oh, stop now! I'm completely sopped!"

    All this time, the demon armies
staring grimly from the wide surround, stood
unamused. Finally, at the recollection
of so many slaves with knives, whose native
bent was to sympathize with outcastes,
the gods regained sobriety, and thought
that they might reason with the misguided bride.
"You don't know what you're choosing. That there
is Skinny Boy, Ghostface, Lefty,
Leperskin." "You can't tell from here,
but they say he smells bad too."
"Oh and the unending drone of gab!"
"He's a babbling, sanctimonious little fool."
"And don't think that's all. He hasn't got
a single slave to earn him pay."
"He'll be in the poor house soon, on the dole."
"We've got palaces. He lacks a proper home."
"He eats nothing but a little sandy spinach with his rice."
"That's why he's shriveled to a mess of skin and bones."

    Little Mother answered them, and, as she spoke, a sea
of memories seemed to break in waves upon her mind
from many lives lived in times before:
"But there is sweetness in him, and in that place;
I cannot say how pleased I am
by the softness of his gestures, and the beauty of his face.
You think he is a fool to give up gold
to seek an aery, insubstantial grace,
but the goal of every pleasure is enduring peace,
unruffled as the still surface of a pool.
Perhaps it is my youth, but I prefer

wild fancies dreamed by such a boy
to fountains full of jewels or seas of coins."

    "He is excommunicate." "He has violated
our entire clan by eating with polluted men
whose shadow should not even
cross his empty plate." "He
has done obeisance at pariah women's feet."

    "You say he breaks the rules of rank;
you, as I have heard, were less fastidious
when he drank up the swill and saved
all things from death in poisonous tides.
As your own scriptures tell: you cannot fulfill
obligation by drawing simple lines
of who deserves respect, what fellowship is right.
Only someone with no capacity for shame
could honestly maintain that duty is defined
by narrowing the normal empathies of daily life,
to segregate each group from all the rest,
to press the miserable down further
in their miserable place. The culmination of all good
is not blind loyalty to the clan or to the state,
but the refusal to cooperate with pain –
and that includes the laws by which you reign."

    Saying these last words and trembling
with anger at the hypocritical gods, the Ethereal, the Unreachable,
the Goddess called Night of Love, and Night of Death,
set off again to leave behind divine
community and to ascend the lonely place.
The gods were silenced by the learning of the child.
But, after a while, recovering their poise, they followed,
at a distance. Now their feelings for the girl changed.
Fear, esteem, and even care, muddled up
what once had been mere lust. Thinking

how they didn't wish to see her hurt,
some tried to alert her to the risk and cried,
"But Howler, Face of Famine, Lord of Sorrow—
he will not accept a wife. Not you, not anyone";
"He is sworn to chastity and some abstract sort of life";
"Goddess of Tears, he burned Eros himself
to bodiless ash. Come back to us."
But she rebuked the well-meaning mob:
"Don't you dare follow me from here
or you will know what fury
an outraged goddess can release—
for I will have the aid of all your wives.
You promised at the start that you would not
dispute my choice. Now it is made,
and there is nothing more that can be said,
by any voice, in blame, or even praise."
So, as the crowd retreated (with slow, wandering steps)
and returned home in deference and in dismay,
the newborn goddess, Mother of All,
through Heaven, took her solitary way.

VII
A Dialogue on Love and Duty

༄

After hours crossing the long plain,
and climbing up the mountainside's steep slope,
she reached the shelf of stone where a boy
practiced stillness of the body and the soul. He stood
on his right foot, the left drawn up
above the knee, his arms twined like vines
before his half-closed eyes. The Goddess,
Plentiful, took up the same position;
she stood, immobile, facing Poison-Drinker,
like an image in a mirror; one male,
one female, but otherwise the same:
in height, hair, feature, frame—like twins.
For days, she stood this way, ate only
air, and concentrated on the soul.
When the Friend woke from his trance and saw
this girl displayed before him,
he wondered to himself, "Who does
this person think she is,
to come here uninvited, install herself
inside my home, and mimic me in yoga?
Alright, let's see how well she copes
with a harder pose." The God of Anger rose
on one toe, raised the other leg,
his knee bent, the toe pointed forward,
then tilted in. His arms reached
toward the sky, and curled around,
as if he wanted to embrace the sun.
It was a frozen moment of the dance.
This too Little Mother mimed,

and stood, motionless, without a sound.
They held the pose so long that snow
settled on their faces, shoulders,
in their hair, but neither flinched.
So the God rocked back onto a heel,
stretched his right leg high into the air,
until it pressed tight against his cheek;
his hands reached up to grab the arch,
and extend the spine, till he stood straight and still
as spears butted in soft earth by soldiers
resting or at mess. His twin assumed
this posture too, and stood, for days, with just
minutest bend and slightest sway—
like a thick, deep-rooted tree—
when battered by hard blasts of wind.
In anger and frustration, he tried a fourth
position, and a fifth—but she matched him
in every balance, every bodily twist.
Each one, they held for hours or days,
or even weeks; they did not eat,
or sleep, or take a moment's rest,
but continued to play out this silent rivalry
of disciplining mind, perfecting form.
And though she had no practice in the thing at all,
she held a thousand postures without a flaw.

The God of Tears at last concluded the event
and settled on the floor, like a lotus on its pad.
He sat, without speaking, and gazed
at this strange, exquisite, nameless girl.
Flustered by his silence and his stare, the goddess
mumbled nervously, "You need not fear.
I am no enemy." Then she felt
immediate distress at what she'd said.
"Now he thinks that I am a complete buffoon.
What clod believes that the Conqueror of Death,

who could defy the united strength of gods
with all their troops and weaponry,
would quake with terror to see that I
can balance for a week on my big toe!"
Her face and neck flushed red,
like the surface of a river, just at dawn,
when the women and the men come down
to bathe on different sides of a sharp bend.
The Friend, noticing her consternation, replied
with a teasing tone and teasing smile,
"Perhaps you are the greatest enemy of all."
She had no sense that what she'd said
was right, that his heart quivered in fright
each time he met her eyes or glimpsed
the smooth surface of her upper arm, discerned
the delicate, strong shape of calves and thighs.

Drawing up her courage, and ignoring both
his remark and smile, she said,
"I have come to practice discipline of mind.
I understand that you despise no class
or person, but accept within your circles:
slaves, outcastes, demons, even girls."
"It is, we think, a sin to scorn fellowship
and learning due to sex or some haphazard
feature of one's origin or shape or skin.
After all, if some lunatic, naked
on a mountain top, with uncombed hair and snakes
for pals — if he can sign a chit for membership,
do grounds remain to justify excluding
some poor citizen born to cobble shoes?"
"You are making fun at my expense."
"But what I said was true, or mostly true.
And, you know, perhaps I wanted to impress you
with my wit." Hearing this, she turned
her eyes down to her feet and did not reply.

THE DEATH OF THE GODDESS

So the Lord of Dreams took up the thread again,
this time more soberly. "You see,
when the central doctrine of your faith
teaches that all the myriad souls are one,
how can you say this chum
of mine is god and this one too –
but in that other group, there's none."

      "I have come to be your disciple."
At this, Oddball snorted loudly, and replied,
"But we have no gurus here.
Indeed, I have just learned from you."
"I'm sure that you have wisdom to impart."
He laughed again, with some embarrassment.
"If you had come here long ago,
I would have said, 'You are quite right.
I have much to say of great profundity
and vast consequence!' A little later,
I had slightly changed my tune,
and would have told you, 'I believe
that I am on the very brink of fine discoveries.
Soon I shall close up the final link
in a universal theory that, I think, may change
the lives of gods, and demons, and of mortal beings.'
But now I hardly see what you, or anyone,
could learn from me, except bland trivialities,
untested guesses, standard clichés, vague
hopes, inconsequential gossip – this
accounts for the entire stock of what I know."
He smiled sweetly, and she thought how odd
it was to hear this flimsy boy
speak of past vanity with as much disdain
as a decrepit, hunched old man. Then,
moved by the gentleness of what he said
and, even more, intoxicated with
his comeliness of form, the goddess wished

to take the god into her arms, press
his face against her breasts, and practice discipline,
not of yoga, but of tantric sex.
She thought, "His eyes are beautiful as black clouds
arriving at the end of a dry season."
But she, instead, assumed an analytic tone,
and said, "Perhaps, living alone with brutes
who cannot speak, but only touch, and look,
and play, and hearing your own words
or silence echoed back each night
and day from caves or mountain sides, you have lost
the sense of what has value in your thoughts
and the lineage of ideas that you preserve.
For centuries, I slept within my mother's womb,
this mountain range on which
you practiced meditative rules.
And all that time, you exercised the mind,
to understand both duty and release.
Now it is your obligation, for those
who have not learned before, to unlock
the store of what you know, and teach."

Swayed, not by her conviction, nor her argument,
but by the sweetness of her speech, the God of Dreams agreed.
"Ask and I will answer what I can.
But I can't promise you that much of worth
will come from following such uncertainty."
And, so, Little Mother of All began.

"First, before anything else,
I need to know, who, truly, is
the greatest enemy?"
"Whoever is held dear
by the gods, or by the people, for there
is never any end to such a person's
vanity, and fear."

THE DEATH OF THE GODDESS

"Who, then, is the greatest friend?"
"Someone who fulfills the final jot
of duty in your regard, but nothing more –
that is not the greatest, but the only friend."

"What is the gravest sin –
for that, above all else, I wish to shun."
"To undermine the goals – however silly they may seem –
that give shape and meaning to a person's life,
or to deprive someone of confidence
to act on what they know is right."

"What, then, is the greatest virtue?"
"To worship God in those the gods despise.
All other virtues, in turn, arise from this."

"Who, exactly, are the gods?"
"Only those who think they are divine
and have the force of arms that can compel
others to affirm the claim as well;
or those who never let themselves
live amid the slum of Earth, and Hell."

"What is Earth, that I have never seen?"
"It is, first, the pain of birth, decay,
and death, and, second, the pain of witnessing
some who claim that they belong to Heaven."

"Tell me, what is this Heaven?"
"It is believing you have followed Right,
though, since the start of time, no human,
and no god, not even any
devil cursed with unremitting Hell,
has managed, or intended, to fulfill
more than the smallest part of duty."

"And what is unremitting Hell?"
"It is a constant misery of the heart
that revolts the gods and all of humankind,
and is not reviled by lunatics alone,
and scattered demons of the lowest sort."

"What makes up misery of the heart?"
"It is compassion, of which virtue
and bondage are both the outcome, and the start."

"When, just now, you spoke of virtue,
I could not say precisely what you meant."
"Many acts and habits of the mind define
virtue, but first, it is the absence of defilement."

"Explain, then, what persons are defiled?"
"In daily life, in love, in work, we
wax to maximum corruption and grow
to be as fully vile as we can.
But the most corrupt of all is the Religious Man."

"So, who is the Religious Man?"
"The man whose eyes are blinded by illusion,
but who claims to see the True with certainty."

"How would you define 'illusion'?"
"Illusion is just this: the absolute sense,
pervading everything we think and feel,
that grades of quality and rank are real."

"Does Illusion ever end? Is it eternal?"
"Its dissolution has a name at least.
The ancient sages called it 'peace.'"

"Where can peace be found? –
Or how can it be made into a real state?"

THE DEATH OF THE GODDESS

"Peace is a word only, a mere sound.
Throughout the three worlds the thing itself
has never found a medium or a place.
There is no peace—for all
the gods and, whatever they might think,
all humankind and even all the demons
live mired in illusion's slop and stink."

When the Friend closed his eyes to meditate
once more, the Goddess of Night and Tears,
of Love, of Death, of Beauty made a second choice.
This time it was exile and purgatory.
Though she assented to the fact that order is a fake,
she knew that this was not enough.
Recognition must saturate the air
in which one breathes, suffuse the light that strikes
the eyes, whatever shape one sees,
so that everything one thinks, each
action that one undertakes, is drenched—
like woolen wraps in heavy rain—
with unqualified, spontaneous disdain
for rank. With that one thought,
she disappeared from the Friend's side, despite
the love that made her long to be his bride.

Patrick Colm Hogan

VIII
The Theophany of an Untouchable

೨

Though Little Mother of All was gone,
The Friend found that his own friends increased.
Many devils came to talk with him
about the nature of the mind, and the prospects for release
from finite life. He replied to everything
they asked, listened when they criticized
or extended what he'd said. But, in his view,
the chances for success were always slim.
The others were more hopeful, despite their state
as criminals, prostitutes, and slaves. Each meeting
would extend to hours in unresolved debate.
And when they all had left, returning to their cells
or streets, or masters' homes, he sat alone
in a vast world he had come almost to hate.

Once, when the demons scattered in the eight directions,
due to rumors of police and a tip about a raid,
the Friend remained behind, silent and disconsolate.
In the distance, he heard tha-tha of a parai.
Then an aged woman's weak voice
called out, as a conch shell sounds
to herald the arrival of a king. But here
the cry of warning was required by law,
so that the heavenly beings and the priests,
nobility, and wealthy men could in good time
retreat behind closed doors, shutter
windows, cover grains they had exposed to dry—
for even a pariah's passing shadow
would corrupt the food of those who were divine.

THE DEATH OF THE GODDESS

The dull thud of the drum and the rasping cry
came near and faded as she circled slowly
up the mountain path. At last,
she neared the spot where the God of Dreaming sat,
but stopped at a respectful distance; she knew that it was not
her place to come too close to lords.
He saw her now, old girl;
Her face was shriveled like dried fruit, and black
as kohl, her hair, thin wisps of greyish
white (like clouds) beneath the cowl
of an undyed robe. She knelt, and set
her stick aside, then lay down, prostrate,
on the ground and prayed. "Fearless One,
God of Fire and Rain, though I am despised
at every level and in every world
I have come to offer what I can. They say
that you are greater than all the other gods combined,
but that, still, you are the most kind."

      The Friend was embarrassed to hear the woman's prayer
and said, "I never asked to be adored.
I never looked for praise. Please – go."
He did not anticipate the flood of sorrow
some dozen thoughtless words could cause.
The woman shrieked in anguish, tore
at her dress, beat her head against the ground
until she bled, then cried, "So,
you too would deny me.
In the course of my long life, I have begged
each god to accept what I could give. I pleaded
with Right Arm of the Faith, Protector of All,
and have been unprotected. Approaching Golden One,
I was refused all wealth. I called
to Thunderer, and my land was struck with drought.
I sought out spirits of the air, yet
the only breeze that touched my skin was loo –

then Ritual Fire, but no flame would take
the offerings I made, and I have passed through
winter with just cold ashes in the hearth.
I tried the Goddess of the Waters too,
but the rivers were mere fissured beds
of clay when I approached to bathe or drink.
The God of Love led my husband to the arms
of dancing girls when I appealed to him.
Death mocked my offerings and took instead
my only child as servant or companion
in the land from which no one returns.
Each day of life, I sought devotion,
and each day another god denied me
all beneficence, until my time
on earth was stripped of any compensation
for the miseries of birth and age.
I pleaded with the priests to intervene,
but they fled in panic at my words;
they locked their doors, and fortified their gates;
even from a distance I could see their dread
that mere proximity of speech would bring pollution.
Of course, they never griped when, every day,
I'd scrub their shit from the latrines.
Then Kali, my friend – she hauls the crap away
once I've scooped it out into her cart –
told me that I should find the God of Dreams,
Image of Hunger, Lord of Rags and Ashes.
He, alone of all the gods, will welcome
any stranger in his home, and answer
any prayer with unqualified compassion.
I see from this that she was wrong,
for even you deny me. Now
there is no other god for me to try."
Saying this, she got up from the dirt,
and turned to re-descend the mountain path,
her hands and face still trembling with hurt.

THE DEATH OF THE GODDESS

When he heard the woman's story, the Giver of Joy
felt a tightness in his heart and nearly wept.
He called after her, in a breaking voice – "Mother.
I did not mean to keep you from my home,
such as it is, or to deny you whatever I can give.
It's just that you are mother and should not
bow down to me." "Instead," he added
(pausing to be sure that this is what he meant to say),
"I should be the one to worship you."
 "You would worship such a thing
as me, reviled in every aspect and relation,
no more dear to gods or men than poison
from the primal sea?" "Mother, no one
has ever been more worthy of my reverence."
The Friend approached and bowed to touch her feet.
But when he brushed her sandal, she began
to change. Her hair stained black and flowed
over her shoulders, thick as the holy river, her skin
grew smooth as melting ice, her lips
red as blood or berries; the single cloth
slipped off her head, unfolded from her waist.
Her breasts were like the snow on mountain peaks,
her body supple as spring streams, her nipples
dark as thundering rainclouds. The Lord of Dreams,
unbelieving, touched her once again:
"Night of Love. Night of Death," he whispered,
"Mother of All. Forgive me.
Until now, there never was an age
when even I acknowledged your earthly forms."
And from that moment, the greatest of the gods
surrendered finally to love.

IX
Memories of Forgotten Wars

❧

For eons, Little Mother and the Lord of Tears
met the poets and philosophers of Hell
in a hidden place, concealed from the paranoid gods,
the national police, and ingratiating narks.
Slave of Time was the most devoted of the group.
Queen of Beggars and the Friend loved him the best
as well. Depending on the day or time, the physical
conditions of the place, the mood that can
pervade a gathering of women and men
(as a sentiment pervades a poem),
or the topic of debate, they felt he was
their younger brother, or their comrade, or a son.
One day, he came to them alone,
deeply troubled by a vision, or a dream.
"It bears on our debates. But, if it's true, it seems
to make them all mere idle talk."
The Friend replied, "Tell us whatever you have seen."

"I was wandering on a battlefield.
For as far as I could see, the floor
on which I walked was thick with corpses.
Hot blood still spilled from them
beneath a gauze of steam in the cooling air.
First, it flowed, then oozed like pus,
from countless severed limbs, pierced trunks.
Here, it gathered to a small, curdling pool,
where a dozen heads were cut in quick succession,
and poured out their fluids, like water
to a sacred font. Over there, it formed

a rill, trickling down the rise that marked
some enemy's front line –
the first three men in an assault, each
took an arrow directly to the heart
(I could not help but think a shameful thought:
what marksmanship there was on the archer's part);
these men, who sacrificed continuing life
so that their nation could brand its name
on a tiny square of land too small to farm,
all fell by chance into one heap,
and so their blood funneled to a single rut,
and flowed along the already sodden earth.
Each place I walked, it was like this;
just the pennons changed, the heraldic crests
painted on the shields, the helmets' feathered combs.
Finally, I came upon a woman, alone;
in her right hand, she held a sword;
in her left, a mace, and on her back
she strapped a quiver of spears, already used,
and then retrieved, with stains from human bowels.
Her hair was stiff with crusted blood;
shreds of blackening flesh, splinters of white
bone flaked off her face
like make-up she put on
too thickly and for too long.
Her eyes were crazy and set back
in deep oval sockets of bruised skin.
She had stripped off the outer breast-plate
and the leggings of her suit, and stood knee-deep
in muck wearing only that long coat
of mail, so I could see, through bores
of chain, her breasts and vulva, and they too,
and all her other parts, were stained in gore.

"Though most of those piled in thick heaps
across the field were dead, sometimes a lingering soul

let loose a stray, pathetic moan,
or shifted slightly to relieve a wound.
This warrior found out each soldier
that still lived, and put her boot down
on his head, and pushed her sword into his throat,
until it snapped the neck and spinal cord;
sometimes she used her mace to crush the skull
against a rock. I followed her throughout.
Forgive the absurd simile, but it
seemed like marching through a field of meat.
Three or four times, I held the branch
of some indifferent, flowering tree and puked;
the last time, I thought the guts themselves
would heave into my mouth.
Finally, the sounds of life declined,
then disappeared. For a time, she stopped
and listened for more shifts, more sighs.
Hearing none, she continued to a brook
far from the main battlefield but still
riddled with the dead, for many wounded men
had dragged themselves onto the bank and tried
to drink. Some died because of wounds,
but others drowned; that, at least, was quicker.
She cleared herself a spot, sat down,
began to clean and polish up her sword.
I wished to ask her many things:
Who were these men? What
was their crime, if anything at all?
Was she Havoc or was she Mercy
that wandered through the field giving death,
as nurses give medicine or water? And what will happen
to these soldiers' children, and their wives?
But one word only passed out
between my lips into a question: 'Why?'

THE DEATH OF THE GODDESS

"'I will tell you something,' she said.
'Perhaps it will answer what you ask.
Bhava, my firstborn, and my favorite –
though I prized all my sons and daughters
for their different quirks and smarts – was still a child;
his face was smooth, his voice clear and high.
And in every part, from the broad form of his skull
to the fine contour of his foot, all witnesses
agreed that Bhava was a most beautiful boy.
One of the ruler demons – though then
I thought it was a god – wanted him
as a slave. I pleaded for his life. I begged,
in fact, that my own soul be sent
to Hell three centuries in exchange
for Bhava's liberty throughout
one normal span of mortal life.
I wept, and pleaded: it is not right,
it is not just, it is a violation
of the moral law and of both our obligations.
But the demon answered with disdain,
"Just who are you to call on Duty with such piety?
Does your delicate sense of obligation
extend beyond decorum, self-justifying
lies and bribery of the gods? I know
you want the child to comfort you in age,
to bathe and feed you when you've grown addled and arthritic,
then, after you have died, to offer
yearly sacrifice and to pass on
your name for seven generations until
you yourself are born again –
perhaps in that same family and home –
after your own punishments in hell
which you've calculated, I believe, at four centuries or so."'

"She paused over the scene, and then went on,
'Each one of us agrees that goodness

is the single source and measure of all things,
that nothing anywhere is greater, or as great:
not all the myriad gods combined
make up one particle of duty.
Each one of us agrees as well
that nothing, either transient or eternal
is more beautiful in substance or in form than Right.
Without duty, they say, there would be
no point or order in the three worlds,
no stability or balance in relations,
nothing to curb the terrors of the will.
But when we turn from the profession to the facts,
we find that, in all worlds and at all times,
no one honors obligation in their acts.

     "'In heaven, the gods laugh at the pursuit of ethics
against will: 'What we do
is moral law; what we desire, itself
defines the moral urge; what we choose
to say creates the universal precept;
beyond the gods, there is no duty –
it is another name for what we are.'
Any god who does not concur
they simply count a fool and spurn.

     "'On earth, as always, things are worse:
if some man acts by duty,
that makes grave danger to the state,
upsets the natural order, and so
perhaps his ribs are broken with stones, or bats,
or jackboots – cracked until they pierce
the lung, and then he drowns in his own blood;
after this, maybe his shattered corpse
is strung up on the city wall – around
his neck a placard reading, "Enemy of the People."
If a woman follows what is right, that undermines

the home. Sometimes, police line up
to rape her in her cell, or soldiers in a bar or street.
The story circulates that she went mad
and inflicted all the injuries upon herself.
No one asks just how she could inflict
repeated rape by 20 men –
she is a demoness; anything is possible.
There are, of course, official statements and reports.
But in the end the memory fades into an epic
of the one eternal war – Good vs. Bad –
and all the past is then deformed like figures
mirrored back from a buckled looking glass.

"'Don't you think this battle too
will be recalled throughout the worlds
as a massive, historic triumph of the Good?
I woke young boys from sleep,
dragged them from their mothers' arms.
First, we bound their hands behind and hauled them,
backward, by the wrists, to hang from trees.
We hoped the screams would reach their fathers' ears.
If that failed, we then tied up
their little pricks and filled their guts with tea.
You can imagine the result. You see, you cannot beat
the little ones too much. They die.
In the end, each one of them gave way
and told us where their fathers hid –
or else the men came on their own. Still,
when their blood had not yet dried on the field,
when the mothers, wives, and sisters had just begun
to grate against the air with their sharp
keening cries – already, in glorious couplets,
like twin steeds bound to a single car,
bards sang of me as the sole foe
of evil in a corrupted world, as defender

of the one true faith, as saint,
as savior, as god incarnate.

    "'In all the worlds, it seems that only demons
retain some memory of obligation – of speaking
what is true and abjuring violence.
And so, if some inhabitants of Hell begin
to practice Right, if a few of them
follow out the homely duties of a child
or spouse, the worldly duties of a citizen or friend,
a general imperative to be sincere or kind,
the others weep, in pity, tears of blood.
For at any time or place only
slaves know the terrible results of Good.
Devils are damned eternally, no matter
what they do in any life,
in any incarnation or any
ghastly, insubstantial wanderings
between one death and a second birth
(slipping into their new form
like a hand into a new glove)
never to have freed themselves from –
Oh, it soils my lips. I will not say it.
In any case, this makes their dwelling
Hell. Hell is in each one of them.
Whichever way they go is Hell.
For there is no penance by which they can win
freedom from that cloying sentiment,
the curse of demons, their eternal sin.

    "'What the apparition said of me
and all my kind, that day he came
to steal my child, was true. But soon
I knew he was demonic, not divine,
for when I wept again, and begged for mercy,
he bit his lower lip, and turned his head,

and cursed me in a breaking voice, and left,
alone. Each demon is damned to recall
all things established at the start.
Even waters of forgetfulness cannot wash
memories of compassion from a devil's heart.

    "'But later, gods came — and men,
for whom my weeping was only added joy;
they savored it like spices in a stew
or honey thickly spooned onto fresh cakes.
The gods went off with my first boy;
the men stole my first girl.
And from that time I vowed to shield
every other child I might bear,
against the unfeeling gods, and sadistic man.
So I have taught them every day
to crush the first soft shoots of fellowship
that grow like weeds in human souls,
to pull up sympathy by the roots,
unless they wish to live their little lives
harnessed and whipped like oxen at the plow,
or used for kicks and then despised, like prostitutes.'

    "At the end, she stood up from her seat
and stretched to her full height until
her figure loomed above me, gargantuan
among the flames and ruins and steaming heaps
of faceless dead. She turned to leave.
Then I awoke, at last, from this vision, or this sleep."

    The Lord of Tears stood gaping at the terror
of his disciple's dream. And Slave of Time
asked, his voice quivering with hope and fear,
"Dear friends, is this indeed the truth?
Is cruelty the basic principle of life?
Is ahimsā just a fantasy, or lie?"

The Giver of Joy was speechless with the shock and awe.
Then the Unreachable Goddess spoke: "That
was not a dream, nor a mystic vision.
It was memory of your years living in the mortal world.
I too recall the persons and the scene.
While our dear Friend sat in meditation,
I walked with you along the battlefield.
But you are wrong to think it was one day.
It was thousands and thousands of days, the same,
but differing in small matters of detail:
the shape of forces, the generals' and the nations' names,
the precise weapons used, their different rates
of murder and of pain, the visible properties of place,
such as the color of the soil before
the blood began to stain, like wine
spilled out across a tablecloth.
But each aspect you describe was there,
each element, every cry,
each couplet sung by lying bards.
Even a hundred thousand deaths and births
cannot erase such memories. They are a part
of everything one does, like a bruise on the heart
that aches with each contraction and release.
But there is one thing that you forgot
Pain is not the raw feel alone.
It isn't mere experience,
just the moment of the act.
It is memory, expectation, and desire.
Pain is not absolute Now,
when, say, the knife first cuts the skin.
It is the memory of the threat, the look of an assailant
who might just as readily have been a friend,
anticipation of a blade plunging to the hilt,
then of the jerk and pull, the hot swell
of one's own blood against one's hands,
then the drag of moments until death,

that will itself cut short all your imagined
future plans. This thought in turn
carries in its wake a huge tide of regret—
for what we once experienced as mere
routine muddle of ongoing tasks
now becomes unfinished lines of future
life, like verses stopped, before the rhyme.
So, you forgot our main recurring theme:
Throughout the three worlds, attachment and attachment
only is the one enduring source of pain."

The Friend smiled softly and replied, "I too
did not recall the point. You have exceeded me
again." "It is not that at all.
You know as well as anyone:
My paean to detachment is insubstantial
as this mountain air; it is mere
common wisdom, got off by heart
like lessons for examination;
it has no force or consequence
in a world where a single man's contentment
rests on the misery of a thousand djinns."
"Yet you reminded us of what
we had both almost forgotten:
Detachment is the aim of discipline,
the only means to persevere in duty
and to achieve even a momentary peace."
After a pause, he whispered, "Goddess,"
and bent to touch his forehead to her feet.

X
Cruelties of the Ruling Classes

❧

After this, Little Mother of All
descended once again to earth. She passed through
many births – and, under many different
names, in different times, taught means
of discipline and duty. In each of her
last dozen or thirteen mortal lives,
she was hauled away by thugs
and murdered to preserve the well-being of the state –
once, she was unburied meat for hungry dogs;
once, she was fed hemlock for corrupting boys;
once, she was stoned as an adulteress in a public street;
once, she was buried, living, in an unmarked grave;
once, she was sold as a slave, and then erased
from every record kept about that time and place;
once, she was denounced for sorcery, and burned at the stake;
once, she was the subject of strange medical trials –
just how quickly does a vial of white
phosphorus burn through the eyes?;
once, her wrists were slit and the Governor
apologized that he could not forestall her suicide;
once, she was left to rot inside a secret
cell, and everyone remarked how queer
it was that she had simply disappeared.

Each method of decease was different from the last;
it expressed, like certain forms of art,
the peculiar cruelty of that ruling class –
and yet all methods were the same as well.
Sometimes there was no trial. Sometimes

there was a trial, but the accused was not allowed
to say one sentence in her self-defense.
Sometimes she could address the court, but
every word was refuted by eye witnesses,
through testimonies paid for by the state or some elite.
In each case where the death was public
and official, the prosecution won over
the hearts and minds of all the people. However
well-beloved she was before arrest,
at the process' end, confused by the official lies,
and bribed by promises of preference,
her friends and followers outgrew
her strange, dangerous, heretical views.
Indeed, when, after months, they took her from her jail
– sick, starved, filthy, and smelling of stale
sweat and piss – battalions of police had to be called,
not to protect the executioner,
but to preserve the victim's life until
she reached the block or scaffold, or the tinder
where her fire would be lit.

        Her final sermon, in her last spate
of days on earth, was – like that
of every other life – delivered to
a group of workers, lunatics, and outlaws
that formed her only friends and partners in debate.
They met in a rented room well off the road
to eat – it was a feast day, and in the street
the children doused all passers-by
with bright crimson dust and sanguine dye.
Then they retired from the stifling heat into
a rose-garden, damp from the light spray
of tumbling fountains blown by the wind.
It was late into the night, but all the friends
who walked with her through rows
of flowering, scented shrubs, and most of all

the former slaves, did not want rest,
but wished to follow through the central question,
which they'd pursued before, but to no conclusive end:
What leads a man or woman to be free
from the incessant wheel of false pleasure and pain?
She knew that it was not so simple
as to contemplate the unity of souls and thereby
realize some transcendental state.
So she said to all her friends instead: "You've heard
from childhood on that every human soul
is animated by four overarching aims:
riches, romance, goodness, and release.
Scholars of the ancient texts professed
that, at least for those not from the proper caste,
pursuit of wealth is lowest on the list.

"However, what the priestly exegetes
too often fail to note is that
wealth also is what lays the ground
for attaining any of the other goals.
No man or woman can contract to wed
without the price of priests and gowns; no couple
can live without the cost of home;
no parents can raise children without the funds
to pay for sons' and daughters' food and clothes.
And no matter how two souls
feel drawn to each other—as the mind,
in myth, is drawn to the Idea of the Good,
or those imprisoned in dark caves are drawn
up toward sunlight and clean,
clear air—hunger rubs the skin
to rawness, so that any hold feels
like attack. Repeated wear of need
erodes even the strongest bonds
of love to slight, spidery strands.

"Worse still, without necessities of life,
no man or woman can fulfill
even one small part of duty,
and no one can achieve release.
Obligation is of three main kinds:
the universal duty of non-violence and truth;
responsibilities dependent on one's work
(no moral law requires cobblers
to cure the sick, or doctors to repair their shoes);
finally, commitments from one's status in the home—
as father, mother, sibling, spouse, or child.
But an ill-fed man, who serves as slave
to a courtier or merchant, overweight
with bulging moneybags, cannot fulfill
even the smallest shred of obligation
to his parents, his children, or his wife.
How can such a slave comfort a mother
in old age, a father who is frail,
and yet is still required to labor in the field?
Where will he find means to cure
his children's sicknesses or give them
all the food they need for growth? His work
itself entails no moral good,
for the very structure of the thing is drenched
with violence—and thus there is no question
of following, or deviating from,
the unique duty particular to his trade.
The foundation stone of obligation is ahimsā —
the refusal to cooperate with harm.
The work of slavery, then, is the very paradigm
of wrong—not only for the slave
and master, but for all who acquiesce as well.
Indeed, whenever a nation permits slavery
in any degree or form, explicit
or concealed, and in any of its parts,

there is this one, unnoticed cost:
the innocence of all its citizens is lost.

"The same ideas could be repeated for release.
The woman begging in the streets, the man
who scrapes into the mine from dawn to dusk
and never sees the light of day, the girl
who works a loom for fourteen-hours, cannot
engage gurus to teach the discipline of yoga,
practice postures, purity of diet and control
of breath, or sit alone in a secluded place
to fix the mind on One and contemplate.

"Every soul is born to life carrying,
from former times, a pattern of what is right,
a shape of good that it can feel, as the hand
that plants can sense soft coolness
of fertile earth beneath its probing touch.
And like the seed that, placed in proper soil
and rain, sprouts and hardens to its one unique
perfection of a tree – like this, each soul,
in right conditions, would grow into its own
outlandish purity of moral being,
and we would see, across one million
persons, one million realized ideals,
each differing from all the rest, each
expressive of its own strange potency
and circumstance, yet all alike in beauty,
as if a million rāgas were played on a million
instruments, by a million masters of the art.
And yet in every eon of historical
time, society has starved each impulse
toward the good, and fostered in its place
desire for group power or for private gain.

THE DEATH OF THE GODDESS

"War, famine, murder, torture, theft—
all forms of cruelty pervade
the world, as you see every day.
Thus both duty and release are made
impossible by the very social forms
reputed to ensure the common good.
Until there is fair sharing out,
until there are no fault lines
of degree and kind, until incomparable minds
are no more named 'divinity' and 'fiend,'
until the very categories are erased,
no soul will reach to duty or release."

She stopped and for a while they did not speak;
then one, named "Slave of Time,"
posed the question that troubled every gaze:
"But how can we abolish slavery or war,
and reapportion wealth to lift the soul
up to purity from the killing floor?"
The goddess could not give an answer.
She did not know, and Slave of Time
saw the look of sadness in her eyes
at the thought that cruelty and pain would never end.
Just then the soldiers trampled through
the thick hedgerow of blood-red roses
and dragged her to her final earthly trial
and death. She vowed to be reborn in human form
only when she learned to answer this demand
and give the people more than pretty dreams,
followed, first, by disillusion, then despair.
For countless years, she, the God of Tears,
and their queer lot of friends meditated and discussed,
but none could see a way to stop society
from stifling all impulse toward what is Right,
as a crazed mother might take a pillow to its crib
and suffocate her sleeping child at night.

XI
The Death of the Goddess

❧

By then the evil age arrived and waxed,
almost unnoticed, to terrible ripeness.
The savage acts of gods and humankind
multiplied, like vermin on a corpse,
until the two societies sustained
entire sciences of horror,
and no field of knowledge was more advanced,
no business was more lucrative,
than fabricating reams of agony and death.
With this the gods felt universal threat.
They saw that, one by one, each aspect,
element, and source of life that once maintained
its independent shape and force, was now
reduced to all-consuming cruelty:
the bond of parent and child, husband and wife,
sister and brother, friends, neighbors, peers,
in time each one of these became
a conduit to inflict more pain.

Thus, gods recognized the decadence of time,
saw the prospect of demise, began to fear
a culmination of their lurid acts;
there were panicked rumors of account,
and the advent of a universal Hell –
a reciprocity of pain, where gods
would find themselves the prey of each precise
enduring agony that they had caused
as they created luxury of things.
Then one or two recalled the nectar,

and they cried out again to Grandfather,
demanding that he follow through his promise of division.
Life Shaper knew also that the time
had come and sent a convoy to retrieve the drink,
though he also knew that it was all deceit—
for immortality from nectar was a fake.
Yes, mortality, that rules the earth,
would never conquer gods who drank ambrosia,
but this victory was won by sleight-of-hand,
for all that is, including death,
would soon dissipate in utter end.

 While gods sat drooling for their fix,
the massive urn was borne above the ground
on a double cross of foot-thick planks
by one hundred of the darkest demons.
Their shoulders stooped; the muscles of their arms
and chests bulged and twisted in tense knots;
their feet cramped; each step
pressed hollows in the rock as if it were
soft clay or mud or oozy sand;
their necks swelled in throbbing surges;
blood trickled out their ears and nostrils—
as they strained against the weight of an eternal promise:
false hope, heavier than the collapsed mass
of stars. And yet, this one service, the Satanic
crew did willingly. For they knew this was the end;
the perfection and the ecstasy envisioned
by the gods would turn to chaos, then
to terror, then unmitigated nothing.
And what was this cipher of stuff
and spirit to a slave, but the casting off
of chains, the dissolving of the neck-clamp and the whip
into a blank space of forgetful deep,
as if one moved from nightmares
into a dreamless sleep.

The nectar had been concealed inside
the center of the earth, and the bearers toiled
out through miles of narrow tunnel
with little air and with no light at all.
It took them days to haul the cargo up,
responding to the call of gods and the order of Immensity.
After a week – first the brief descent,
then the struggle upwards, feeling
their sightless way, shoulders and cheeks
scraped raw against the tapering shafts –
they turned a hairpin curve,
and, suddenly, they faced the entrance of the mine,
a hole of brilliant light sliced into dark.
When they emerged into the company of gods,
they were blinded by the sun, broader than a demon's
fist, and by the glimmering waves of sea
that rose to the horizon on three sides,
and by white sand stretching from the cavern
to the shores, bleached garments of the gods,
their gold, their glittering jewels.
The hurt was like a stab of needles
that pierced the lens and jelly to the cradling cup.
Some flailed their arms against the beams;
some wheeled like drunks and stumbled from the path,
their hands pressed tight against their eyes;
some tried to stuff their faces in the sand –
anything to block the ache of sight.

The police, though demons too, reined in
the riot of their peers with lead-tipped canes.
They had another task, to build the ceremonial
stage and altars to three hundred million
gods and goddesses; they stacked entire
forestsful of wood for fires, and made
huge towers from which sacrifice
could be performed according to the ancient rites

visible to all the congregation of the blest.
When work was finished, the devils were dismissed.
Some shrieked for joy of freedom, however
brief, and quickly fled to re-unite
with family and friends in paradise of Hell—
for the ditches of Gehenna were now in flower, and the air
was filled with sounds of water tumbling over stones
and with the scent of lilac or of jasmine, or of rose.
But others—enslaved so long
that they could not remember their own homes—
lingered around the edges of the stage,
uncertain where to go. Finally,
the gods, alarmed that they still stood
on holy ground and might pollute
some sacred thing, drove out
this straggling, sad, disoriented few.

So, this final, tiny crew of demons
fled for an ancestral place they hardly knew
and long ago had ceased to miss.
But one djinn, Slave of Time,
as he descended through the earth into
the third of the three worlds, that was his home,
felt a sudden stab of hurt, as if
the dais, and the nectar, the struggle out of caves
and into light, the threats of raving gods,
had exposed some still raw memory
borne over from past life.
When he entered into Hell again,
after eons of forced labor, exiled
in a hostile land, and when he heard
the pattering of streams, and smelled the flowering
jasmine in the garden by his long-abandoned home,
he recognized at last just what
this strange sensation was that caused such pain:
compassion. Many lives lived in constant

shame had strangled any feeling of solicitude;
not through detachment that leads to peace,
but with stifled vengeance pressuring the chest, like coursing
blood blocked by clots inside a valve.
Now, on the last day, the strain against his heart
had waned, the muscle and the inner wall repaired.
But he remembered a goddess's demise, and—although he stood
at home, in an infernal hermitage, where
the scent of rose-hedges suffused the air—
beneath the strong branches of a blossoming tree,
this finally unfettered slave surrendered to despair.

In heaven, the deities assembled before the stage,
gazing with hope and worry on the massive urn.
Noticing two empty places in the crowd,
one of the lowest and least consequential
of the gods—with no devotees to speak of,
no shrines; and he was hardly even mentioned
in the sacred texts—this godling ventured timidly,
"Don't you think we should request
the twins, beautiful as dawn above the ocean,
to find the Goddess of Tears and God of Dreams
and deliver, with respect, our invitation,
requesting their auspicious presence at this feast?"
Some laughed at the idea; others shouted,
"He had no part in drawing out
the nectar." But the little fellow felt emboldened
by the fact that greater deities responded to his words
at all, so he continued in his reedy voice,
"Neither did Grandfather, and Right Arm of the Faith
stole every drop—but they are here.
And Conqueror of Death saved us from poison."
The God of Exact Rites, the Father of Sacrifice,
stood up in the assembly, to pronounce
precise rules for this high ceremony:
"My daughter, once called 'Virgin Goddess,'

may join us – though only if she repudiates her spouse.
This is something I, and the joint chiefs,
have always urged. She can be redeemed.
But her husband brings disgrace on all of us.
He has soiled himself with outcastes and has become
unclean." The minor deity was silenced, and ashamed.
There was no more dissent
among the gods and goddesses. All
found the final argument complete.
For no crime is more loathsome
to the deities of any place
than betrayal of the caste by someone born
to their own master race.

   When he heard of the debate among the gods,
the Lord of Dreams frowned and admonished his Ethereal
Beauty, Night of Love, Night of Death,
"You absolutely must not attend this summit.
They will just revile you in gross terms,
when you refuse to disavow our bond."
"But my father has arranged the feast,
and no one else will say that he
disgraces everyone who recollects
the poison and your sacrifice." "It is
attachment only that leads you down
this path – wounded pride for our exclusion.
Do not think of that, but stay
and we will weigh again what can be done
to make society kinder to the mind."
She smiled and replied, "Excuse me,
my little husband, but I believe
you do not mean a single
thing that you have said. You dearly hope
I will attend the feast, to denounce my father
and all the other gods, to praise my Oddball" –
here she pushed a curl of stray hair

away from his left eye—"to show
that when I chose to share a life with you,
it was no fluke and no mistake,
and that I never did nor would regret
refusing their vast stores of gold
for a skinny boy sitting on a cliff.
Yes, I will go—and say
just that. You see, in one thing
you were entirely right: Attachment,
a vice I endlessly decry,
is indeed what draws me to this affair.
But you are wrong to think it is my pride.
It is just my love for you—Pretzel-Legs,
Count-My-Bones"—she touched a finger to his ribs—
"Little-Dollop-of-Ingudi-Oil," and though
she joked, there was a sort of sadness in her voice
when saying this. "I will go,
and I will say to anyone who hears,
that for a fourteen-year-old child,
I was wise beyond my years
to choose the finest husband from the godly peers.
You are the only one among the manly
gods, who reveres his wife—in the same degree
and kind—as he is, himself, revered by her."
Saying this, she scrunched her fingers up
into a tiny inch, to tease her boy,
and smiled again, though now her voice
was breaking with emotion. Then she touched
his cheek gently with her opening hand.
Tears welled up in the god's eyes
and for the only time in his eternal life,
he was ashamed. "Forgive me,"
he said, "I have sinned against a friend."

Now, gods quaffed great bowls
of nectar at the feast. All that the sea

had given, they consumed – until
their bellies no longer fit
inside their belts, but bulged to tight,
round, sloshing drums above their trousers
or their skirts. As they drank, belched, laughed,
sang out obscenities, stumbled
giddily around the altars, heaved
beside the sacred fires, and rose from dozing off
in grime and pools of their own bile,
night fell on the last day of time.

    Little Mother walked among the scented gods,
reek of booze mingling with sweet perfume;
their golden robes were loose and billowed
in light breeze; their crowns, necklaces, and rings,
thick with diamonds large as a man's hand,
shimmered in the firelight like stars.
Their bodies were brushed with lines of sandal paste
in festive patterns, but these now smeared
and ran with rolling sheets of sweat
across their arms, chests, or straining guts.
The robe and veil in which the goddess draped herself
were made of moonlight and the stuff of dreams,
though they seemed to be a weave of silver thread.
The wasted gods called out to her
in vulgar words, although their jaws were numb
with poison of the drink and their speech became so
slurred that the Mother of All
and Last-Born Girl could not quite
say precisely what it was she heard.
The leering sots did not make out
the features of her face, but greatly liked
the breasty shape that they discerned beneath
the single wrap of dress. Moreover,
she wore silver, and not gold,
which made them think that she was poor,

and thus an easy mark – for fancy words,
or jewels, or threats against her husband's job.
As she passed closer by one howling bunch –
looking for her father or the Great Immensity himself,
to announce that she would not agree to their conditions,
though that meant death by forfeiting the drink –
a fair divinity, blond as sun,
grabbed her by the hips and pulled her close,
tried to bite her lips, and pressed his crotch
against the fine pleats of her skirt. But,
before he could undo the knot of string
around her waist and throw her to the ground,
she spat into his face and snarled,
"Don't you know that I am Everything-that's-Fierce,
that all my days are spent among
the dead and dying, that I dwell in every
burning ground and every burial place,
in all the slums, and with the homeless in the streets,
that I work in the tannery and the latrines,
that my devotees and friends include
all those the gods despise as base,
that you would class my husband Untouchable
and outcaste from your exalted race?"

She realized at once that this was her farewell,
her final speech. She had imagined grander things
– a trial unfolding on the central stage, with prologue,
formality, debate, with many truths
revealed about the cruelty of godly rule.
Instead, the end was this: a sordid scuffle
on a weedy corner of the lot, where the suitable path
of well-cropped green gave way
to scraggy mess, a sack of obscure night,
an unattended sideshow with a cast
of addled goons. And she saw too
that there would be no grandeur in the pain.

THE DEATH OF THE GODDESS

Yes, when it comes, it is a brute
and ugly fact, valueless, and unredeemed.
That she had learned a dozen times before,
and yet, each time, she managed to forget.
"I too have been a fool," she thought.
And so, before surrendering to the horror of events –
the working-through of a predestined plan
to miserable and squalid ends – she sought
to calm her heart, that fluttered like a flame, and feel
that same detachment that she had always taught.

A band of red-eyed gods approached,
in fits of snorting laughter at what she said.
"Let's take a look behind the drape, and see
if she has well-used knees, like all the scrubbers
of latrines." "And whores!" They giggled like pimply teens
until they belched and nearly choked. Then
they tore the clothing from her body and the veil from her face.
The cloak slipped easily from her head,
her breasts, her hips. As it fell, dissolving
into some other māyā, it revealed,
beneath, the clean but ragged clothes of sweepers
and, on her skin, the shameful marks of a pariah.

Seeing this, the gods recoiled in horror
at the crime they had committed with this act
– not in violation of a goddess, but,
they thought, in some pollution of themselves.
Then their fury rose against the thing before them –
she had no drum, and called
no warning for those ahead to screen
themselves from her approach. Her presence
on the grounds alone was desecration of the sacred
law and every rule of social good.
"We are all fouled by the touch
of unclean clothes, and spit, and skin."

"What can we do now to punish
her, to free ourselves from sin?"

     Fearing that one or two members of their band
might have some qualms about the needful act,
and then infect the rest, one god,
more sober than his friends, set out,
to end debate before it could begin:
"Somewhere within her soul, she too
must wish for penance, purity, and release.
Our holy writings teach one thing
above all else: ideal order
keeps everyone in their right place.
To permit a breach of structure is to risk complete
collapse and the end of peace for every class.
You all recall, a servant boy confessed
that he had read the sacred works, and sat
in meditation, pursued advancement of the mind.
You all recall how Right Arm of the Faith
beheaded the impious fraud right there,
as the child sat on the ground, unarmed.
Perhaps you do not know that even as
his head fell from his shoulders to the earth,
the slave's lips formed these grateful words:
'Oh, Redeemer!,' he prayed, 'Today, you saved
a delicate soul from misery of grievous sin.'
This one too will thank us, in the end:
her voice will sing with gratitude above the fire."
In this way, a shabby crew of gods concurred
that a goddess must die on the sacrificial pyre.

     Then she, whose smallest particle
encompasses all things that live and die,
was dragged across the sacred plain where gods
had danced, and fucked, and broken drinking bowls,
and spilled their guts, and pissed; the shards

of vessels cut her skin, until she trailed
a dozen lines of blood through dirt;
the wash from pools of urine stung her wounds.
The impious gods bound the battered girl—
her feet and hands together, like a wild deer
killed in a hunt—and hauled her upside-down
onto the highest platform of the tower.
There, they enacted all the proper rites,
to regain purity for those who are defiled—
made the gestures, said the words that purge
contamination from the body and the soul—
then they heaved the Goddess high into the air
above the massive fire. This entire
pageant, this theatre of terror, she permitted,
and did not once resist its progress,
for she knew that all this cruelty must
spend itself before the violent dream,
that stretched through every eon of material time,
could finally end. But, to show that, even
then, they did not break her will,
when falling, she called out
against the crowd of gods—who stared and munched
as if they watched a circus act—
and against her father, who had organized
this systematic vice, an outcaste's prayer
to the God of Tears. Just then, the Sacred Pyre
crushed her to his breast. At first, her body jerked
against the piercing tongues of flame, then
she seemed to tremble, and softly turn in currents
of scorched air above erratic waves
of fire; after some time, her arms
and legs drew in against her breast
a single, slow movement of obscene grace,
like a flower closing from a sudden loss of day.
When a timber cracked that held the flames in place,
she tumbled to the path in a rain of glowing embers

that flared brightly for a moment in the air, then,
as they fell against her, faded to white ash:
a veil of new snow to hide her face
and, for what else was left, a silver sash.

So she who was once most beautiful in all
three worlds became charred skin
stretched tight around a brittle frame,
a shriveled knot of ravaged flesh;
like an unborn child, tiny, rounded to a ball,
mantled with white soot—a winding sheet, or caul.

XII
The End of Time

&

First, bewildered silence, then shattering of peace.
A company of fiends crowded space
around the pyre, howling like rabid wolves;
deformed djinns and hideous demons cried,
cursing the holy violence of gods.
There were pariah-dogs everywhere,
their teeth bared, dripping venomous spit;
they circled around the sacrificial place
and kept the gods at bay, for fear that they
would desecrate the goddess' resting form.
The forests pulsed with a constant, angry hiss
of snakes, and monkeys' panicked shrieks.
Each tribe of beasts heaved out
their sound as if they aimed to chant the goddess' name
and thereby call her aid to ease their pain,
as a man whose wife has died might wake at night,
in haze of sleep, and seek the solace of that same
wife's embrace – reach through the sheets
to her accustomed place, but only find
appalling shapeless space where she had been.

On hearing this agony of nature, the God of Tears
knew right away the cause, and before an image
or a formulated wish could take shape in his mind,
he was standing at the edge of the defiled ground.
The snarling bitches who stood guard
licked his feet in sympathy and with respect
and quietly stepped aside to let him pass,
then closed ranks again behind,

more tightly than before. The God of Tears
saw none of this, but, oblivious to all surround,
knelt down beside the huddled form.
Though feeble from a thousand centuries of penance –
he remembered how she called to him
"Hello, Count-My-Bones!," "How
is Knobby-Knees, today; how is
My-Little-Sack-of-Ribs?" –
though now reduced to a mere scaffolding of man,
when his body shook with shock, with terror, and with grief
all earth and all the heavens trembled.
Then he gathered in his arms the little that remained,
and, holding the charred corpse tightly to his breast,
caressing what he thought must once have been her face,
he spoke in disbelief with halting words,
"Not one hour ago,
this ruined corpse was God."

Then the Lord of Yoga wept. He
who had preserved the three worlds from poisonous death,
could not protect one girl alone,
whom he loved most.

"Because, among the beings born or made
or merely thought in godly sleep, I loved
and I admired only you, so
you were the only one I could not save.
'Throughout the three worlds, attachment and attachment
only is the one enduring source of pain.'
I see now this was a warning aimed
at me – a warning that I failed to heed.
And so, above all else, it is
my sin that has permitted this."

The gods pressed in, nudged, pointed
fingers, exclaimed, asked, burped, picked,

scratched, and ogled. It was quite a sight.
Crazed with sorrow, unmindful of the munching crowd,
he took the ragged corpse up in his arms,
gentle with the strands that bound this clutter of charred bones
into a single, tenuous, remembered form.
Cradling her frail neck between his shoulder
and his cheek, he tried to recreate the postures
they had made the day they met,
as if mere repetition of the act
would change that memory to present fact.
So, he balanced on one toe,
and curved the other leg around her waist
and stretched their arms above, in curls,
as if they would embrace the moon;
he held her crumbling hands against her hips,
like the Cowherd God chiding his devoted girl;
he stretched her right leg high into the air,
and held it with his left, and turned
her broken face up to his lips, and pressed
her tattered ribs against his breast.

    Initially, his step was slow
from one position to the next, but then
his pace increased, to one continuous act:
exquisite agony of dance. But that
was not the end, the speed continued to advance,
and, with it, the movement's force. The gods
reacted to the change at first with mild alarm,
then growing fear. The edge of the Remover's heel
speared land, and all earth shook;
then, the ball and ridge of his left foot
struck down and sent broad cracks
across the surface of the heavenly spheres.
At this, the gods, who had known dread
just once before, were terrorstruck.
They scattered from the place in panic,

and trampled one another down, as they
had done when running from the poison.
Then, like frightened foolish children
who fear the consequences of their pranks,
pretending that the sacrifice was just an accident,
they pleaded with Immensity, the Source of All, "Restore
to Little Mother the form and soul that lived
before her fall, for the violence of the Mad One's
grief will otherwise destroy us all."

  Here, as before, the Shaper of Life and Death
turned to his beloved son for help. But now
the Eternal Ally, who was once supremely confident,
stood muddled and uncertain on the trembling ground.
For many centuries, he was sick and almost mad,
and his arms, legs, and chest, that used to be
both muscular and fat, had withered
to sharp bones in sagging folds of skin.
There was no trace of any of his former wealth.
He gave each penny of it back
to slaves—for they're the ones who mined the gold
and fashioned things of beauty to his taste.
He thought, "Why did I believe that it
belonged to me?" He wandered, naked, homeless,
like a mendicant, remembering his dear wife,
how he had made her pass a trial to prove
that, as a prisoner of war, she was not raped;
how he had still abandoned her, with an unborn child,
in wilderness, alone, to quiet the salacious crowds
who cried "Adulteress!" when she returned;
how, when they met again, he publicly proclaimed
he would accept her in the palaces again,
if only she would prove her chastity a second time;
how she refused, and leapt into a cleft of rock and dirt
welcoming at last the unreserved embrace of Earth.
Each time this history passed

across his mind, he wept, and whipped his back
with chains, and cried out, "I have sinned."
So, when Grandfather asked for aid in this,
he answered, "What right have gods to live?
Once I, like all of you,
reviled the Lord of Tears for his queer life,
for his obsession with the state of slaves,
for the respect he gave to the ideas and the aspirations of a girl.
But, finally, which one of us was right?
In structuring society by rank
according to imaginary grades of good
we have destroyed ourselves, and spoiled
whatever might have made community worthwhile.
Now, my only fear would be
that the Friend is too kind to let us die."

Such a thing was never said before
in the congress of the gods. Violence had not once
been named in proper terms. Since the start of time,
each leader pointed to the heart of darkness
at the center of divine society and called it—Beauty,
Justice, Truth. The Beloved Son was the first
to break with this tradition of deceit
(for Oddball had been outcaste from the start).
So, his admission, addressed to Grandfather, before
the full assembled clan of goddesses and gods,
was catastrophe for māyā. It was as if
the center of the stage fell in and all
the characters who lived before our eyes,
were reduced again to actors and to actresses—
for merit and degree make up the paltry
frame on which each ruling fancy shapes
its world of terrifying dreams.

From this collapse of universal lie,
the final metamorphosis began.

THE DEATH OF THE GODDESS

The Goddess grew immense and million-headed,
her million mouths stained red with blood
of all the past and present generations –
of humans, demons, gods, birds, beasts,
and every living thing since the start of time.
The Lord of Tears overwhelmed with bliss
greater than he had ever felt before,
knew that all the gods had been outdone.
He lay down on the still-smoldering ground,
placed his head beneath her foot, a sign
of her supremacy, and prayed: "Oh, Goddess,
before husband or wife, parent or child,
before the crowding mass of men, before
all 300 million gods, before
solidity of space, persisting time,
the elements or churning sea, before
the cycles of the day and night,
familiarities of touch, distances
of sight, before sleeping and waking,
before sensual delight, before wealth,
before even duty, before release,
you were, and all that is, was peace."

The gods did not dare speak. They trembled,
waiting. Then Grandfather, Immensity, Great Origin,
spoke for all; pressing palms together
before his face, he bowed low in reverence:
"Goddess of Eternal Night, Fierce One,
Destroyer of Illusion, Ma. Forgive us.
You are the final death, greater than all,
conqueror of worlds. In the end,
each soul succumbs to you alone."

But when Grandfather raised his head,
he did not lie beside his estranged
child, and he no longer faced

the goddess and the girl with whom he never fully
reconciled. Instead, before the eyes of aging
deity, loomed immense transfiguration:
not two, nor one – commingled,
yet distinct in attributes, like
rain in air, or fine particles of sand
stirred up inside a pond, or sea
when it is churned, by nature, or by unnatural means.
He tried to focus on the vision, and saw
that it contained the universe, all planets,
stars, brute matter of the human place,
the concealed lands of demons, the opulent gardens
of the gods. And it embraced, as well,
all time: each age of life's
decline to further violence and misery.
To see it all laid out like that,
as if all days of life were simultaneous,
crowding one another in a small space
of night, like etchings in black sky –
the history of those events, now
branded on the thickening air, pained
his heart with recollection, and he groped
toward glimmering apparitions of eternity,
feeling the weight of a million, million years.
"I have grown old," he thought,
dismayed. Approaching closer to the present time,
he scrutinized the world of gods, now
unraveling from all its multitude of past.
There, he saw the wild beyond the sea.
And in the wild, he saw the hermitage where he
and Grandmother rested. And in the hermitage,
he saw himself, befuddled and alone –
an ancient god, grey and sickly, lying
on a bed of sacrificial grasses.
These faggots were unlit, but
there were fires all around the place;

he tossed his head and moaned, as if in fever,
or tormented by some memory, or dream.
The First God's eyes clouded for a moment,
filled with tears – the smoke perhaps, or,
perhaps, remorse, for all that he had done,
in infinite forms – and when he looked again,
he could not tell if what he saw,
now swaddled in white cloth, was a dying
man or new-born child, or if the bed
where this queer, timeless person hid
was, in fact, a funeral bier or infant's crib.

    Suddenly, Grandfather was weak with thirst.
Heat ate into his brain, like white phosphorus
spilled onto the skull. Looking up,
he saw a thousand suns burned the air
above his head; the land began to scorch
his soles. Desperate for relief, he sought
again that place where the final feast
and desecration had occurred. Now
the area was forfeit to the elements,
and like all the places of the gods,
it too would wear away to scraps and dust.
Thin wisps of smoke still rose
from dying embers where the Sacrifice had burned.
The tables where the gods had sung and laughed
were overturned, the drinking vessels cracked,
stray shards scattered across the field;
as he traversed the path down which our Ma
was dragged, the fragments cut his feet.
He stared in disbelief
as his blood leaked
into red earth
with hers.

It was then the baffling sound arose.
Grandfather became confused—one time
it seemed to be a song of joy, then,
a screech of fear, that pervaded the unending space.
Before his eyes, all history and culmination,
not only of the gods, but of all beings,
dissolved into mere sand and nothing.
The chronicles grew brittle, white ants
ate up the memory of time,
and all that still remained of words recording
what had gone before, he saw dissolve
to film of powder on a shelf where scrolls were stored.
The images that had been carved in rock
were scraped by wind and rain to pitted nullity,
the monuments reduced to curious, cracked
stumps of stone—here and there, absurd,
untended fractures of form among
rough clutter of rubble and ragged weeds.
And, of course, whole histories of speechless
expectations, hopes, ideas, feelings, moods,
that underlie and animate all
movements of the soul—these too were lost.
Even the memory of jostling life that once
filled the air with clatter and with song, in changing
thicknesses across each habitable place—
all this was fading to dull void.
He thought, "Nothing will be left to say,
'Here, men and women loved; here,
gods fought; here, demons played.'"

Then it was the blackest part of night.
Indefinite densities of dark and shade
encompassed him, in what was once a country
of unending day, where he walked
and feasted and made love and ended quarrels,
and listened to the ordered shapes of sound

that made wild beasts weep with sorrow
and calmed the human heart with memories of love.
Recalling this, as if at some great
distance, he heard a sharper tone within
the cry or scream or song that had surrounded him.
It was a flute and some master played
a rāga for the middle of the night.
The rasa of the thing was peace. He knew
at once the player and tried to call.
But the only sound that stumbled from his lips
was the broken name of a goddess who had died.
That was when he felt the cool water
first flowing around his blistered feet
in gentle currents, then his ankles and his calves.
In hardly any time, it reached his knees,
but he pressed on, seeking desperately
for love and music. It flowed higher still,
and he struggled with the lift and weightlessness
and waves, until he came at last
to a broad edge of absolute abyss.
Now, the father of the gods, of every
living being, the source of matter and of form,
was just a minuscule speck
on a vast rush of current in a bankless stream.
The universal noise of joy or pain
became the roar of water tumbling down
to sudden silence and the cipher of all things.
Borne along by the swirling void, Grandfather,
in the final moment before the fall and crash
of nothing, turned upward to the vault of sky
and was just able then to see
a final time
the image that all beings seek
before they die:

The one, transfigured form grew limitless at last,
pervading whatever makes or is made,
all worlds, all ages, all
matter, spirit, sound, sense, form,
idea, all cycles of time, all
impulse and principle, all the living,
each ancestral generation, every
unborn soul, all values,
all agencies, all things attained
and all that has been lost, all
that is remembered and everything that is forgotten.
And when their union encompassed even the Flowing
Spring and Immensity itself, then the dream
dissolved at last to imageless sleep –
No being or unbeing, truth or illusion,
no thought or withering of experience into memory,
no duty or sin, attachment or letting go,
no things the gods revile or protect,
not even the unsheltering void, immense, unbodied.
What is, was darkness concealed in darkness only.

Then Grandfather dreamt.

About the Author

PATRICK COLM HOGAN is a Professor at the University of Connecticut, where he is a member of the Department of English, the Program in India Studies, the Program in Comparative Literature and Cultural Studies, and the Program in Cognitive Science. The author of sixteen books, Hogan's best-known work is *The Mind and Its Stories: Narrative Universals and Human Emotion* (Cambridge Univ. Press, 2003), which was hailed as "a landmark in modern intellectual life" by Steven Pinker of Harvard University. He has published fiction in *The Journal of Irish Literature* and poetry in *minnesota review, Kunapipi, The Journal of Commonwealth and Postcolonial Studies,* and elsewhere. *The Death of the Goddess* was inspired by Buddhism, Indic thought and poetry, and political events and social conditions of the modern period.

Patrick Colm Hogan

Other Books by 2Leaf Press

అ

2LEAF PRESS challenges the status quo by publishing alternative fiction, non-fiction, poetry and bilingual works by activists, academics, poets and authors dedicated to diversity and social justice with scholarship that is accessible to the general public. 2LEAF PRESS produces high quality and beautifully produced hardcover, paperback and ebook formats through our series: *2LP Explorations in Diversity, 2LP University Books, 2LP Classics, 2LP Translations, Nuyorican World Series,* and *2LP Current Affairs, Culture & Politics.* Below is a selection of 2LEAF PRESS' published titles.

2LP EXPLORATIONS IN DIVERSITY
Substance of Fire: Gender and Race in the College Classroom
by Claire Millikin
Foreword by R. Joseph Rodríguez, Afterword by Richard Delgado
Contributed material by Riley Blanks, Blake Calhoun, Rox Trujillo

Black Lives Have Always Mattered
A Collection of Essays, Poems, and Personal Narratives
Edited by Abiodun Oyewole

The Beiging of America:
Personal Narratives about Being Mixed Race in the 21st Century
Edited by Cathy J. Schlund-Vials, Sean Frederick Forbes, Tara Betts
with an Afterword by Heidi Durrow

What Does it Mean to be White in America?
Breaking the White Code of Silence, A Collection of Personal Narratives
Edited by Gabrielle David and Sean Frederick Forbes
Introduction by Debby Irving and Afterword by Tara Betts

2LP UNIVERSITY BOOKS
Designs of Blackness, Mappings in the Literature and Culture of African Americans
A. Robert Lee
20TH ANNIVERSARY EXPANDED EDITION

2LP CLASSICS
Adventures in Black and White
Edited and with a critical introduction by Tara Betts
by Philippa Duke Schuyler

Monsters: Mary Shelley's Frankenstein and Mathilda
by Mary Shelley, edited by Claire Millikin Raymond

2LP TRANSLATIONS
Birds on the Kiswar Tree
by Odi Gonzales, Translated by Lynn Levin
Bilingual: English/Spanish

Incessant Beauty, A Bilingual Anthology
by Ana Rossetti, Edited and Translated by Carmela Ferradáns
Bilingual: English/Spanish

NUYORICAN WORLD SERIES
Our Nuyorican Thing, The Birth of a Self-Made Identity
by Samuel Carrion Diaz, with an Introduction by Urayoán Noel
Bilingual: English/Spanish

Hey Yo! Yo Soy!, 40 Years of Nuyorican Street Poetry,
The Collected Works of Jesús Papoleto Meléndez
Bilingual: English/Spanish

LITERARY NONFICTION
No Vacancy; Homeless Women in Paradise
by Michael Reid

The Beauty of Being, A Collection of Fables, Short Stories & Essays
by Abiodun Oyewole

WHEREABOUTS: Stepping Out of Place,
An Outside in Literary & Travel Magazine Anthology
Edited by Brandi Dawn Henderson

PLAYS
Rivers of Women, The Play
by Shirley Bradley LeFlore, with photographs by Michael J. Bracey

AUTOBIOGRAPHIES/MEMOIRS/BIOGRAPHIES
Trailblazers, Black Women Who Helped Make America Great
American Firsts/American Icons
by Gabrielle David

Mother of Orphans
The True and Curious Story of Irish Alice, A Colored Man's Widow
by Dedria Humphries Barker

Strength of Soul
by Naomi Raquel Enright

Dream of the Water Children:
Memory and Mourning in the Black Pacific
by Fredrick D. Kakinami Cloyd
Foreword by Velina Hasu Houston, Introduction by Gerald Horne
Edited by Karen Chau

The Fourth Moment: Journeys from the Known to the Unknown, A Memoir
by Carole J. Garrison, Introduction by Sarah Willis

POETRY
PAPOLÍTICO, Poems of a Political Persuasion
by Jesús Papoleto Meléndez
with an Introduction by Joel Kovel and DeeDee Halleck

Critics of Mystery Marvel, Collected Poems
by Youssef Alaoui, with an Introduction by Laila Halaby

shrimp
by jason vasser-elong, with an Introduction by Michael Castro

The Revlon Slough, New and Selected Poems
by Ray DiZazzo, with an Introduction by Claire Millikin

Written Eye: Visuals/Verse
by A. Robert Lee

A Country Without Borders: Poems and Stories of Kashmir
by Lalita Pandit Hogan, with an Introduction by Frederick Luis
Aldama

Branches of the Tree of Life
The Collected Poems of Abiodun Oyewole 1969-2013
by Abiodun Oyewole, edited by Gabrielle David
with an Introduction by Betty J. Dopson

2Leaf Press is an imprint owned and operated by the Intercultural
Alliance of Artists & Scholars, Inc. (IAAS), a NY-based nonprofit
organization that publishes and promotes multicultural literature.

NEW YORK
www.2leafpress.org